D1493226

your *Child* and his *Art*

1 What does art mean to my child? (See page 9)

your *Child* and his *Art*

A GUIDE FOR PARENTS
by VIKTOR LOWENFELD

THE MACMILLAN COMPANY · NEW YORK

Foreword

THIS book is written exclusively for parents, yet it may be of help to anyone who has direct contact with children and wants to promote their growth through creative expression. The book discusses the parent's role in the promotion of creative activity at home. It discusses how the parent can help his child in overcoming his difficulty. It provides the parent with information regarding the connections between the art of the child and his personality growth. It deals with proper art materials and also with the space which we should provide for the art of our children. The book actually consists of answers to questions from parents, collected over a period of six years on my lectures from coast to coast. These answers, brought in logical sequence, are based on the latest available research, on teaching experiences, and on a wide range of observation. The answers deal with average children and no attempt is made to use art as a therapy for abnormal cases or as a substitute for any necessary clinical counseling. It would be entirely against my feeling and desires to make the home the place for it. On the contrary, throughout the book, the contribution of creative activities for the child's happiness and for the home has been emphasized.

v

The book has been organized in such a way that questions which deal with the meaning and understanding of child art, and how it can help parents in bringing up their children come first. How parents can contribute in helping their children to express themselves creatively comes next. A discussion of important questions referring to the different age levels and stages of development makes up the main part of the book.

The book is written in such a way that parents should be able to refer quickly to the question which most directly relates to their child, without having to read the whole book.

Contents

Illustrations

7–10 YEARS

10–12 YEARS

your *Child* and his *Art*

a word to all parents about
their children's happiness

I HAVE seen children surrounded with an abundance of toys, crying, tense, and unhappy, not knowing what to do with them, unable to use their minds and imaginations to achieve happiness. I have also seen children completely absorbed and content with a single piece of wood, using it at one time as a train, and at another zooming it through the air, as an airplane. What is it that makes one child unhappy in spite of all apparent advantages, and another happy and content without such advantages? Happiness apparently does not depend on such outside influences. It grows with the child's disposition, just as all other character and personality trends do. A child's happiness depends greatly on the environment in which he grows up, and particularly on the understanding of the parents for his needs. Love alone is not enough, especially blind love. To remove all obstacles may not always be to a child's advantage. To give the child all he wants may too often mean depriving him of important longings, the gateway for discoveries and explorations.

The fulfillment of all wishes takes away the initiative to search for satisfaction. It should be kept in mind that the fulfillment of a child's "outer" wishes is not always connected with the satisfaction of his inner needs. A child may be restless and nervous, unable to remain "occupied" for any length of time. Recognizing this inability, the parent may provide him with as many "changes" as possible, if only to avoid the continuous whining of his child—at least for a short period. Such a child's needs are not for more changes or toys; rather they are for increased love and understanding of the wide range of experiences of which he is capable, but which have been neglected in the child's past, thus inhibiting him. To give the child more toys may only add to his restlessness. He may be interested in a new toy for a short time because of its newness; but, incapable of using his own imagination for new combinations and usages, the novelty of the toy will wear off quickly. Nothing has been done to satisfy the inner needs of the child. If a child has a rash caused by a food allergy, it is senseless to put an ointment on the rash. The rash may disappear for a short time; the allergy, however, will remain, and is not actually cured. In order to help the child, in both instances it is important to find the cause of his disaffection. Restlessness consists of inability to sustain attention, whatever the cause may be. We usually cannot remain with one thing if our interest becomes exhausted. Yet the more we can see, feel, and apply our imagination in general experience to one thing, the more will our interest be evoked. To develop this great variety of sensitive relationships constitutes one of the main needs of the child.

There are people who need a continuous flow of excitement. If they don't have it, their life is dull. They have become insensitive to the richness which surrounds them. The continuous search for new excitement is then rather an escape from their own inability to deal with themselves, their own imagination, their own world. It is the same escape which we foster when we give a restless child more things with which to play. We have offered him more excitement, but nothing to help him solve his own problems. The child has a world of his own, and the sooner we help him realize it without imposing our own adult standards on him, the better he will develop.

The growing number of emotional and mental illnesses in this nation is frightening. The best protection against any such occurrence is the early recognition of our child's needs. While we are most apt to recognize his physical needs, we greatly neglect his emotional and mental needs. We are full of concern if our child has a fever, if he lacks an appetite, or if he loses weight. While his physical growth, his health, are most important, there are other components of growth equally important for the happiness of the child and also for his happiness as a future citizen. How the child uses his mind, how he uses his hands, whether he reacts sensitively toward what he sees, hears, feels, or touches, whether he develops desires to communicate with others, are all part of his happiness. It is up to you to develop the sensitivity which is necessary to recognize the child's needs when and where they may occur. This book should give you a better understanding of such needs through one of the child's most natural forms of expression—his art. Thus it should serve two major purposes: It should help you to understand your child's art activities and it should also provide you with the ability to see in his creative activities some of his major needs which otherwise you may not have discovered.

why is it important that
my child creates?

WE cannot readily answer this question without putting ourselves in the position of the child. Let us try to "look through his eyes" and actually find out what goes on in Johnny's mind while he is busy with his painting.

First of all, when he begins he must think of "something." Often this "something" seems to us insignificant. For the child, however, it always means a confrontation with his own self, with his own experience. As he "thinks" of it, his thoughts concentrate on the experience to be painted. His thought process, the ability to think and concentrate on something, becomes stimulated. It is an important part of the initial step in creative activities. Let us say that Mary wants to paint "how she plays with other children in the yard." It is self-evident that Mary will include only those things which she knows and which are important to her. Important to her, however, are only those things to which she has established some more or less sensitive relationships. For Mary, the apple tree in the yard may have big buds because she was watching them grow. Johnny was using the tree only for climbing; buds had no meaning and were therefore not included. Johnny was interested in Mary's dress. He likes Mary. His painting indicates more details on Mary than elsewhere. From that it becomes quite clear that his painting is not an objective representation. On the contrary, as we shall see, it expresses his likes and dislikes, his emotional relationships to his own world and the world which surrounds him. It then combines two very important factors: his *knowledge* of things and his *own individual* relationship toward them.

In order to understand fully these two factors, let us for a while go back to our own experiences. We, too, can only recall things to the extent to which either our knowledge or our individual relationships permit us. Let us think of a traffic light. We all know that it consists of three different-colored lights. Our knowledge has registered that. We will, however, not be so sure with regard to the location of the colors. Is the green light on top, or the red? Once we have become sensitized toward this particular location, we shall incorporate this newly gained relationship into our permanent understanding. Such sensitive relationships can, however, be fostered by experiences which we have with things. If I, for instance, were color blind, I would depend on the location of the lights, and would very soon become aware of the red light being on the top. Needless to say, the more sensitive relationships I establish, the greater is my understanding and the richer is my life, for what is true about the traffic light is also true about flowers, trees, and all that surrounds us.

Mary, therefore, has given us an intimate understanding, through her painting, of the type of relationships which she has established to the things which she represented. As she grows, these relationships change. She will know more about things, and her emotional interest will also shift. The greater the variety in her paintings, the more flexible will Mary be in her relationships.

As Mary continues to paint her back-yard scene, she adds things according to the significance they have for her. Perhaps the swings on the apple tree come first to her mind. She loves to swing on them. But there is Joe. She does not like him because he always teases her. So, according to her likes or dislikes in color or placement, she gives expression to her dislike of Joe in her painting. Because he is stronger than she is, she can never show her dislike directly, but in her painting she can. She can do many things in her painting which she could not do otherwise. She feels better afterward, just as we feel better after we have talked over an important thing with a good friend. It bothers us to keep things all to ourselves, to have them "eat into us."

Virginia was a girl who was very tense. She did not want to talk. She did not draw because whatever she drew was not liked by her parents. She was afraid to stay alone in a room, especially at night before she went to sleep. This continued over a long period until one day she could face her difficulty in a drawing, which, together with the assistance of an understanding teacher, relieved her from her anxiety. This, of course, was a gradual process which could take place only after she had won confidence in her own means of expression, and was thus enabled to face her difficulty. This is what happened. Apparently quite some time ago, just before she fell asleep one night, she saw something moving in her room, moving toward her. She was sure that a person was in the room. She did not want to move. In the morning, when she told her parents, she was informed she had had a bad dream. But it occurred again and again, stimulated by a shadow caused by a moving street light. Gradually, Virginia became tense and full of anxiety. Nobody knew why, until her teacher encouraged her to draw and paint freely. This was not only good for her present condition, but it also provided her with a flexibility which was necessary for the ability to face her past experiences in her creative work. It occurred quite spontaneously. As she grew able to face her own experiences, her tenseness and anxiety diminished and gradually disappeared.

This would not happen to Mary, because Mary is used to expressing whatever comes to her mind. As she continues to paint her background picture, she fills her whole page. Unconsciously she distributes things so meaningfully that her painting almost appears to be organized. Indeed, much organization took place inside her. What she *knew* of the tree, the swing, Joe, and other things had to be related to how she *felt* about these things, and this had to be related to the *location* of the things. She also gave some definite colors to the objects which she painted. Thus another relationship was established. All this organization takes place in the child subconsciously. But it is all part of Mary's personality. Virginia could not do it. She was too tense and restricted, especially in the beginning, when she was not allowed to express herself according to her own desires.

We must know that everything the child does and to which he is exposed has some influence upon him. If the child in his creative work continuously attempts to relate all his experiences, such as thinking, feeling, perceiving (seeing, touching, and so on), to one another, it must also have a unifying effect on his personality.

As Mary goes on to paint her back-yard picture, she includes Rowdy, her dog, and Dad, who fixes the fence. Mary could not draw Dad without putting herself into his place while fixing the fence. This makes her better understand Dad. It is one of the important attributes of any creative activity that we become more sensitive to things with which we are dealing. If Mary thinks of her environment more sensitively, she has been taught to do one of the most important things that we need in the world today—to become more sensitive to the needs of others. This is one of the important prerequisites for a *cooperative* attitude. But Mary not only becomes more sensitive to the things she paints; she also develops a great sensitivity to the materials she uses. She learns by experience that the lines of a crayon are different if she puts different pressure on it, that she can use the broad side of the crayon, that water color merges easily and produces beautiful mixtures—all this she learns by trial and error, and soon incorporates it into her paintings.

To *discover* and *explore* what different art materials can do, "to learn their behavior," is also one of the very desirable trends which the child develops through creative activities. The ability to think independently and creatively as fostered by art, however, does not remain solely with art. It is a faculty that is used wherever men have an opportunity to strive for better and higher achievements. It is one of the outstanding characteristics of democratic living.

Why is it important for your child to create? It is important because your child should be happy and free like Mary, and not as tense and inhibited as Virginia; because your child, too, should develop her thinking and feeling about herself and her environment as Mary does. Your child's thinking and feeling should never become as restricted as Virginia's; your child, like Mary, should develop into a well balanced human being who uses equally well her thinking, feeling, and perceiving. Like Mary, she should be able to put herself into the place of others to discover their needs, too, so that she will grow up to be a cooperative, helpful citizen. She should freely and independently enjoy discovering and exploring the world around her. Above all, she should feel that she is an individual who stands on her own feet fearlessly, a happy human being.

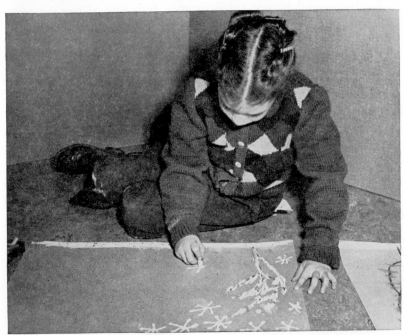

2a, b   A healthy home environment is most advantageous for child art.   (See page 1)

WHAT DOES ART MEAN TO MY CHILD?

In our educational system everything points toward learning, which in most instances means acquiring knowledge. Yet we know too well that knowledge alone does not make people happy. One-sided education with the emphasis on knowledge has neglected many very important attributes which our children need to adjust properly to this world. Art for your child, introduced in his early years, may well mean the difference between an adjusted, happy individual and one who, in spite of all learning, will remain an unbalanced individual who has difficulty in his relationship to his environment.

Art for your child may well be the necessary balance of your child's intellect and his emotions. It may become the friend to whom he naturally turns whenever he has something that bothers him—even unconsciously—a friend to whom he turns whenever words become inadequate.

how do I interfere with my child's art?

THE curious reader may ask why we begin with a discussion of interferences rather than with a discussion of art motivation. I believe that
the greatest contribution which a home atmosphere can make to the art
of children is not to interfere with their natural growth. Most children
express themselves freely and creatively if adult interference does not
inhibit them.

Needless to say, most interference is done completely without awareness, for all parents have the best intentions for their children. Most interference has as its cause the lack of understanding of the child's real
needs. These needs change as the child grows. To put ourselves in the
place of the child is not always easy; in fact it is one of the most difficult
things in education, because it assumes that we know the child's thinking, feeling, and perceiving.

A scribbling child of three years, for instance, may be completely
happy while making scribbling motions on the paper. A parent, unaware
of the child's needs of obtaining better and better control of his movements by merely "practicing" his scribbling, may ask the child, "What
are you drawing?" Since the child may not connect anything but his

enjoyment for obtaining greater and greater mastery over his motions with the scribbling, he may not understand his parent's question and may therefore not react to it. With the best intentions, the inquisitive parent, unaware of the meaning of scribbling, may go on by asking the child, "Can't you draw an apple?" The parent is also unaware that a child of three years does not think in terms of pictures. The child will look at his parent, not knowing what his parent actually means. For the child an apple is something to eat, to smell, or to hold in his hands. It is not something to draw. Drawing an apple is still inconceivable to this three-year-old child. However, since his curiosity has been stirred, he may reply with, "You draw it." Again out of the best intentions to "help" the child, the parent may draw an apple for him. The child in his urge to please the parent now wants to draw "apples" too. He ceases to scribble, and from now on imitates the picture of the apple, which for him is only a kind of "loop," since he does not transfer a picture consisting of lines into a meaningful reality. It may happen that when the parent next approaches Johnny, the child's drawing shows a page covered with little loops. Not knowing what they mean, the parent again asks, "Johnny, what are you drawing?" and Johnny proudly answers, "Apples."

In spite of our best intentions, we have clearly interfered with the child's needs to express himself. We can only understand the full effect of such interference if we realize the importance which creative activity —in this instance scribbling—has for him. Johnny was just about to discover that there is a relationship between his arm movement and the scribbling lines on the paper. Coordination between movement and the effect of the movement is, however, most important for his whole future development. On this coordination of one of his most important senses depends his ability to move about, to develop manual skills, and in addition his language, because here too the coordinated movement of his tongue with the effects it produces are of utmost significance.

We have also interfered with an independent discovery of the child and the confidence which such independent actions give to him. The self-assurance growing out of the fact that he *can* control the line is an important experience. We have no right to deprive him of it, and it may impair his self-confidence for other actions.

We have also interrupted his flexible experimental approach toward his scribbling. We have directed him toward rigid repetitions, thus preventing him from finding out for himself new situations, to which he continually has to adjust. As Johnny grows he may not be able to use creative activity—as Mary does—as a means to express himself whenever he

feels tense or whenever he might enjoy such activity. Had we not interfered with Johnny, he might have continued with his scribbling as one
of his natural activities. It is for this reason that we place interference at
the beginning of our discussion.

ABOUT COLORING BOOKS

Coloring books are the most common means with which we try to
satisfy our children's needs for art activities. Coloring books most commonly consist of drawings in outline which the child fills in with color.
Because they are so easily obtainable in dime stores, they are the simplest
thing to give to children; but we should say, right at the beginning,
that they probably have had a most devastating effect on children and
their art here in our country.

In order to understand the effect of coloring books on children, let
us go through the process a child goes through while using them, and
let us also find out the aftereffect this process may have on our children.

Let us assume that the first picture the child has to fill in is that of a
dog. As soon as the child is confronted with the task of following a predetermined outline, we have prevented him from solving his *own* relationships creatively. *His* relationship to a dog may be one of love, friendship, dislike, or fear. There is no opportunity for him to express his
relationship and thus relieve himself of tensions of joy, hatred, or fear.
There is no place in coloring books to express anxieties such as Virginia
has. There is not even a place for the individual differences of Mary and
Virginia. In filling the outline drawings, they are regimented into the
same type of activity, with no provision for their differences as individuals. Of course Johnny, unaware of all these implications, and by nature somewhat lazy, enjoys coloring the dog; but as he colors it with
crayon he realizes that he could never draw a dog as well as the one he
colors. He may even be very proud when he is through with his activity.
After all, he has colored the dog. Next time, in school or elsewhere, when
he is asked to draw something, he remembers the dog in the coloring
book. Realizing that he could not compete, he says, quite logically, "I
can't draw." (See Figs. 3a, 3b, and 3c.)

I have heard many teachers or parents say, "But my children love
coloring books." This is quite true. Johnny loved them too. Children
in general, however, do not discriminate between things good for them

3a   A child's expression before he was exposed to coloring books.   (See page 12)

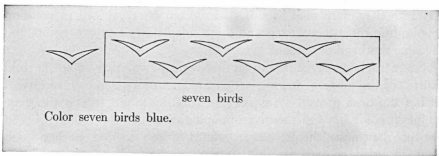

seven birds

Color seven birds blue.

3b   Coloring-book illustration, which the child had to copy.

3c   After copying from coloring books, the child lost his sensitivity, as can be seen **in this drawing.**   (See page 12) 3a, b and c: Courtesy of Dr. Irene Russel and Blanche Waugaman, Research Bulletin of Eastern Arts Association. Vol. 3 No. 1.

or things detrimental. That they love things is not always an indication that they are good for them. Most children prefer sweets to vegetables, and without doubt would always prefer them. This, however, does not mean that we should adjust their diet to sweets. Children, once conditioned to overprotection, love it too. In fact they become so dependent on it that they can no longer enjoy their freedom. In countless cases I have seen parents doing everything for their children—children who simply stretch out their leg and their shoe is laced, then turn around and their hair is combed—almost automatically. These are the children who sit in the midst of their toys and don't know what to do with them, or go to camp and sit lonely in a corner while others enjoy their freedom and play.

A child, once conditioned to coloring books, will have difficulties in enjoying the freedom of creating. The dependency which the coloring book creates is devastating. It has been revealed by experimentation and research that more than half of all children, once exposed to coloring books, lose their creativeness and their independence of expression, and become rigid and dependent.

Some teachers may still tell you that with the coloring book the child learns the discipline of staying within the lines of a given picture (area). It has also been proved by experiment that this is not true at all. More children color beyond the given boundaries in coloring books than in objects they draw themselves. If Johnny draws *his* dog, he has much more incentive to remain within *his* boundaries than if he colors a dog in a coloring book to which he has no relationship.

Thus, it has been proved beyond any doubt that the coloring book makes the child dependent in his thinking (it does not give him the freedom to create what he wants); it makes the child inflexible, because he has to follow what he has been given; it does not provide emotional relief, because it gives the child no opportunity to express his own experience and thus acquire a release for his emotions; it does not even promote skills and discipline, because the child's urge for perfection grows out of his own desire for expression; and finally, it conditions the child to adult concepts which he cannot produce alone, and which therefore frustrate his own creative ambitions.

ABOUT CUTOUTS AND PATTERNS

Much the same thing that has been said about coloring books is true for cutouts and patterns. Cutouts and patterns do not permit the child's own spontaneous expression. They do not provide for individual differences. At Eastertime I visited a second-grade classroom. All around the room were colored, hectographed cutout patterns of Easter bunnies. When I asked one of the children, "Ann, which one is yours?" Ann, after looking around and putting her finger to her mouth inquisitively, said, "I don't know." Then suddenly a glow came over her face and she pointed at a particular bunny. "This one is mine." I asked her, "How do you know it?" She explained that her thumb was dirty and had left an imprint. That was her only identification. I shuddered at the thought that children should be able to identify their own work only by means of spots. I asked the teacher, "Which one is Ann's bunny?" The teacher answered, with a somewhat impatient voice: "I have forty children in this classroom. How should I know which bunny is Ann's!" I am convinced that the teacher had the best intentions. However, not knowing the implications of her teaching prevented her from making a different approach. Actually, such a classroom situation is exactly the type of education which leads toward totalitarian thinking: all the children in the class were regimented in their expression. All were alike. No individual differences were permissible. In such an atmosphere the individual must lose confidence in personal expression. Becoming conditioned to a given pattern, the child expects a pattern at all times. Once the pattern is withdrawn, he feels lost and without the confidence to use his imagination independently.

That cutouts promote a child's skill is as untrue as that coloring books promote discipline. The child who creates his own figures will be more careful to cut out his own predescribed lines than one who cuts out lines which are "dictated" and often misunderstood.

SHALL I HELP MY CHILD IN HIS ART?

Before we can answer the question whether we should help our children in their art expression, we must first agree on what we understand by "helping." We can distinguish between two types of help to our children. Mary may say, "Mother, I don't know how to draw myself picking flowers." If Mother shows Mary "how to draw," she imposes her adult imagination upon her child's. In other words she shows Mary how Mother would have picked flowers, while Mary may have had an entirely different experience related to picking flowers. Flowers look different to children than they do to adults. Through the eyes of Mary they may appear larger, brighter, or taller than through Mother's eyes. Picking flowers may be a different feeling for Mother than it is for Mary. Mother may feel it foremost in her back, when bending down, while Mary may feel it in her arms when reaching for them. Mother may relate different thoughts to picking flowers. For Mother it may be the sad occasion of Armistice Day, when she always picks flowers to put on the grave of her husband; for Mary it may be a happy occasion: she always picks flowers for Mother's Day. Mother has an entirely different concept of Mary than Mary has of herself. For Mother, Mary is a little girl. She *looks* at her and sees her from the outside, as she compares her to other children. Mary *feels* important because she is still a small child and to her everything seems to be centered upon her. She only draws what is important to *her*. She could not find release through her Mother's drawing. Such a drawing is meaningless to her. It provides her only with a substitute for an experience real to her. It does not make her more sensitive toward the flowers, nor toward her own relationship to the flowers. Mother's "help" only serves as a temporary crutch with ill aftereffects, because if Mary has discovered that Mother will "help" her once, she will come again and again for more "help," until she becomes dependent in her art expression on Mother's "help." Even if we work on Mary's drawing just a little, it may have the very same effect as drawing the whole figure. The little "help" we have given her will always remain a foreign body in her drawing. It will serve as a standard to which she is unable to apply the rest of the drawing. Such a discrepancy only creates lack of confidence and finally the "I can't draw" attitude.

We have seen that such "help" only constitutes an interference with the child's creative expression, with her freedom, her confidence; and because it also inhibits her emotional release it may interfere with her future happiness.

If, however, we understand by "helping," making the child more sensitive toward her experience, we call such "help" a motivation for her art expression. "Mary, how do you feel when picking flowers? Do you stand upright? How is your arm? What flowers do you pick? When do you pick flowers? Why do you pick flowers? Have you ever taken a flower apart? What kind of flowers do you like best?" and so on. After such questions Mary will become conscious of many things which apparently did not occur to her previously. Such a motivation, which makes the child more sensitive toward the things she expresses, is very helpful indeed. A more thorough discussion on motivations will be given on pages 27 to 28.

SHALL I CORRECT WRONG PROPORTIONS?

The more spontaneously Mary draws, the less chance there is for her to become tense and inhibited like Virginia. As long as we can nurture this spontaneity in Mary, she will express herself freely and be a happy child. (See Fig. 4.)

As part of this spontaneous approach toward her art, Mary will occasionally use proportions which appear to us adults "wrong." Yet we have to keep in mind that "wrongs" and "rights" change when applied to different things. For instance, it is wrong to wear a bathing suit on the street, but it is right to wear it on the beach. It is wrong to say that what is right for adults is also right for children. This refers to food, sleeping habits, and other experiences. We can say that distant things appear smaller, but they do not necessarily have a small meaning; that is, they may be far away, yet may take up an important space in our minds. Should we then draw things according to how they appear, or according to how important they are? This is precisely the question which pertains to the proportions used in the creative activity of our child. Mary has received her Christmas present, a beautiful doll. For her this doll means everything. It is more important than anything she can think of. If she were to include it in her painting, it would be larger than anything else—it is so very important. Actually, the doll is not out of proportion at all, as compared to the tree or the other things in her painting, because it actually *is* more important than the tree. Therefore we can say that she painted a true relationship.

If we adults say something is out of proportion, we assume that visual appearance, how things look, is the most important factor. Yet we know quite well that often our emotional relationships are much more important than appearance. The child most often does not distinguish between visual and emotional relationships. His proportions indicate the significance things have for him rather than size relationships with regard to appearance. To make something large because it is important is an illusion just as it is an illusion to make something small because it is distant. A distant tree is actually no smaller than a near one. In the same way Mary's doll is not actually larger because it is important to her.

Proportions change as a whole or in parts according to their importance in children's drawings. If we correct them, we interfere with the child's emotional affection for the things she exaggerates.

Should we never correct proportions? As long as the child is satisfied with his expression, we should not interfere with his work. It will only make the child inhibited.

Mary drew herself giving you your birthday present. Full of excitement she was holding a beautiful vase. She was afraid it would drop out of her hands. Naturally, she drew the hands "out of proportion," but it was her *true* feeling that she had when giving you your birthday present. We do not want to correct truth, even if it is of relative value. For Mary, her *feeling* of holding your present was more important than her appearance. To disregard this fact would not only offend her feeling but inhibit her art expression.

If Mary, however, discovers size relationships with regard to appearance, and becomes unsure about certain proportions, she herself will indicate it. "Mother, is the child on my drawing too tall in comparison to the house?" Your answer should not refer to yardstick measurements. Rather, you should try to make Mary more sensitive in experiencing size relationships. "Mary, do you think your child could go through the door? If she were inside the house, do you think she could look out the window?" Such questions would immediately cause Mary to put herself in the place of the child she draws and establish a vivid, experienced relationship.

In conclusion, it may be said that there is no need to correct any proportions in children's drawings or paintings. After all, we are more interested in preserving the child's freedom and happiness than in receiving final products which are "pleasing" to the average adult taste. Further,

4   As long as we allow Mary's expression to be spontaneous, she will reveal herself in her own way. (From "Creative and Mental Growth," Revised Ed.)

22 My child does not relate colors to objects. (See page 91) (From "Creative and Mental Growth," Revised Ed.)

it may be said that the type of proportions the child uses in his art usually reflect their intimate relationships and experiences to the object. Even when we are unable to detect such relationships, we should not risk the danger of offending the child's sensitive relationships by imposing adult standards of "correct" proportions. We have seen that "correct" only refers to appearance, and loses its validity when it is used to refer to expression. As soon as the child develops the urge to find size relationships, this new discovery should be supported by the motivation of experiences which lead to the child's own discovery of proportionate sizes.

SHALL I ALWAYS PRAISE MY CHILD'S ART?

It would be very misleading to think that everything the child does should be praised. There is no reason to praise the child in his art unless he deserves praise. Praise wrongly applied may nullify praise which is needed at a time when the child's self-confidence may depend on it. Mary may know that she did not concentrate at her work and that it is of little meaning to her. Praise would only destroy Mary's confidence in you. In many school and home situations I have experienced conditions in which undue praise has only caused the child to doubt teachers' or parents' sincerity.

How can we protect ourselves from applying false praise? The simplest method is never to praise unless the child's creative achievement appears evident. There are two ways by which this can be ascertained. A spontaneous outburst of the child may be the clearest indication for it. "Mother, look at my barking dog!" This certainly deserves praise. However, not all children are as demonstrative as Mary. Johnny may be very quiet, and never say much spontaneously. We then have to assure ourselves of what Johnny intended to do. "Johnny, tell me something about your painting." If Johnny still does not say anything, we should have to continue our inquiry. "What is this, Johnny?" We should point at something definite in his painting. Johnny would then give a brief account of what he has been doing. "This is Dad washing his car." If this actually relates to his drawing, a positive comment with regard to Johnny's ability to think of Daddy—or whatever the experience is which he represents—would encourage Johnny to think in greater details of his experience. Your praise should boost the confidence of your child in establishing more and more sensitive relationships to his experiences, for the more sensitive his relationships to his experiences, the richer will be his art expression. You can even ask Johnny for more details. "Johnny, show me how Daddy washes his car. What does he use for it? Where is his car standing? Has he closed his doors?" But never ask him suggestive questions such as: "Johnny, where is the sponge? Where are the fenders? Where is the hose?" Such remarks as: "You did not draw the wheels. Can't you add the antenna?" must never be asked.

Unless we give the child the opportunity to discover for himself his own world, our encouragements are destined to be restrictions.

Needless to say, encouragement and praise vary from individual to individual. A child who has been inhibited for a long time, and who did not want to draw at all, needs much praise even at the slightest establishment of a relationship between his experience and his art expression. Mary would not need much praise. For her, art expression has become a necessary part of her personality.

SHALL I CRITICIZE MY CHILD'S ART?

What has been said about "praising the child" applies in even greater measure to criticism. Undue criticism is more harmful than undue praise. Since our criticism is usually based on our adult taste, it will not fit the child's needs. This does not mean, however, that criticism should be avoided altogether. A criticism at the right time should help the child to find himself in his art. If we ask Johnny, "What did you paint?" and he says indifferently, "Oh, nothing," or, "I don't know," don't be satisfied with such an answer. This is only an escape from facing himself in his work. In another instance Johnny might tell you a long story about his painting, but nothing of what he says is expressed, at least not visibly. In this instance ask him about the details which he mentioned but which apparently are not in his painting. "Johnny, you said you are swinging on a swing. Where is the swing? Can you show it to me?" Needless to say, no criticism should ever refer to *how* Johnny draws. Every child should be free to express himself in his *own* manner. However, if you feel that Johnny should know more about a swing than his painting shows, there is nothing wrong with asking him: "Johnny, do you remember how your swing was fastened on the tree? Did you have difficulty in getting on it? Did your legs touch the ground?" Such questions only increase Johnny's sensitivity, and thus serve not only his art but also his relationships to his environment.

It would be completely wrong and harmful to Johnny's self-confidence to criticize his manner of art expression: "Johnny, your swing does not look real," or, "Johnny, you don't look like that." The child expresses in his art *his* level of growth, which cannot be changed or "corrected" through superficial criticism. Growth is a continuous process, and we cannot force the child into it. Since Johnny is not ready to relate his painting to reality, a criticism which forces him to compare it with reality would only be discouraging. For him it is much more important to establish a relationship between his own *experience* and his creative expression. Reality at this point is inconceivable to him, and since it is out of his reach it would only frustrate him.

To look for reality in our children's drawings is one of the most common mistakes. "It does not look real" is the worst thing you can say to a child about his art. That Mary's art does not look real to the adult eye, that it does not look real to you, by no means indicates that it is not real to her. However, the kind of reality is quite different. Reality in appearance does not make things real to your feelings and emotions. Mary's paintings are much more real to her feelings and emotions, to *her* world of experiences, than a reality which is meaningless to her. If we ask Mary to adjust her paintings to our adult concept of reality, we overpower her own sensitive relationships to her experiences only to please ourselves. The result of such frustrating impositions would be as tense a child as Virginia, who is afraid to express herself because she can never please her parents.

There is another very important factor to remember before you criticize your child's art. Avoid criticism after the work has been finished. The most effective criticism is the help you can give your child during the process of working. As the child produces, he grows with his work. Once the product is finished, his interest in it vanishes quickly. Too much emphasis on the final product may stress it beyond its significance. We must again remember that the child does not engage in creative activities to produce pictures, but to express himself. We must also remember that the art expression of the child is not aimed at producing artists. Rather it serves the child as an important means to his growth, regardless of whether *we* consider the creative product "beautiful" or "ugly."

MUST MY CHILD'S ART BE PLEASING?

"Pleasing" means so many different things to different people that it is very difficult to discuss it. Needless to say, "pleasing" usually refers to the individual who feels pleased. We have found that even if we adults were to agree on a standard of what "pleasing" means, our standards would differ greatly from those of children.

The child expresses in his art *his* world by his own means. Mary is different from Virginia, and both are different from Johnny. If they have not been told by adults to produce "pretty pictures," it will never come into their minds, for art expression for them does not mean producing pretty pictures. Whatever there is in a child should come out in his expression. A child who is greatly concerned with the organization of her picture, that is, with the placement of all the objects on her paper and their relationship to one another will be an entirely different child from one who spontaneously paints freshly all things which come to her mind, unaware of any "proper" placing. Which of the two children is better is difficult to say. They are different, and this difference is precious to us. Only in totalitarian regimes are these differences neglected or suppressed. Perhaps the "properly" organized painting looks prettier to us adults. By stressing this factor, and by denying the other child his right for more spontaneous expression, we signify that we are not doing justice to democratic principles.

There is something much more intriguing in children's art than mere external prettiness. The individual who reveals himself in his own way in his art not only can be more fascinating to us; his ability to do so is of vital importance for his growth and development. Let us not impose our concepts for prettiness on children. Children's paintings do not need to please us in their external effects. The art of our children can have no more pleasing effect on us than that of seeing our children grow and be happy through it.

SHALL I HANG MY CHILD'S WORK ON MY WALLS?

For every parent whose child engages in art, the problem arises as to whether he should decorate his walls with his child's art products. This has been born of the widespread concept that the purpose of pictures is to decorate walls. Many people even classify the quality of a picture by the standard of whether it would decorate the wall of their dining room or living room. That this is only a very negligible purpose of art does not need to be stressed. Many of the greatest masterpieces would be completely out of place on the wall of a dining room. Like the artist, the child expresses in his art his relationships to experiences. There is, however, a distinct difference. While the artist's attention is focused on the final product, the child's attention is focused on the process of painting, on the experience he has while doing it. Once Mary has finished her painting, it has fulfilled its purpose and is no longer important to her. To hang her pictures on the wall, therefore, is less for Mary's sake and more for our own benefit. Needless to say, there is nothing wrong if we do things for our own benefit so long as they do not harm our children.

In hanging Mary's painting on the walls we may unnecessarily divert her attention from the experience to the final product, and thus make her more critical toward her paintings. Further, it may take away some of the spontaneous approach so important for her emotional well-being. If we hang a large enough number of her paintings around her room, Mary may not notice this effect as much as if we hang only one picture or even frame it. By hanging up *one* picture, we definitely signify our recognition of, and preference for, it. This may have serious consequences. Mary may want to please us again as much as she did with this picture. She wants to copy it, or at least to imitate its major characteristics. This will prevent her from flexible experimentation. She soon may become fixed in the one style which she created in the framed painting. She may become repetitious, unable to adjust to new situations. I have seen many children who reverted to previous "styles" on the basis of their parents' preference for one particular painting. Even scribbling children may stop scribbling for fear that they will not produce something which their parents would like to exhibit.

Since no definite standard of preference for a particular kind of painting is created by hanging many paintings of Mary's on the wall, to do so may not be disturbing to her at all.

Virginia, however, is tense and afraid to express herself. Now, after much encouragement and strong motivations, she produces a painting. Overjoyed with her achievement, the eager and well meaning parent frames her picture and hangs it on the wall. For Virginia the danger of stopping her work for fear that she cannot please you again as much as with the framed picture is much greater than with Mary. Virginia will hold on to any external success. The problem with her is that she is too tense and controlled and aware of her own actions. To direct her attention to her final product by hanging it on the wall and thus glorifying it may only add to her controlled and tense behavior. We may think that such an action may please Virginia and encourage her to produce more art. No doubt it does please her, but it does not give her any stimulation for new experiences. Let us not forget that the stimulation for more creativeness and greater flexibility does not grow out of the art product but out of a greater sensitivity toward experiences. Since we did not provide Virginia with new experiences, a glorification of a particular painting may only block her in her development and encourage her in imitating her successful painting.

The framing and hanging of single selected paintings is definitely harmful. The hanging of many pictures, however, is left to the discretion of the parent and his knowledge of his child.

how can I foster my child's art?

THE question "How can I foster my child's art?" is the same as "How can I promote my child's growth and development, my child's flexibility, his ability to adjust to new situations, in fact, his happiness as a human being?"

The child's art expression is only a documentation of his personality. If his personality is, like Mary's, free, happy, and uninhibited, his art expression will be free, flexible, and uninhibited. If his personality is, like Virginia's, tense, restricted, and inhibited, his art expression will also show the same characteristics.

To promote free art expresson, then, is the same as providing the child with a free and happy childhood. Needless to say, nothing can ever replace the love of parents, and only parents can provide this for their children. So whatever we say in regard to the fostering of art in our homes is said with the thought that love must be present at all times.

Basic to all art expression are the underlying experiences. Without them no art expression is possible. These underlying experiences are found everywhere. To grasp them, to develop a sensitivity for them, to capitalize on them, are the privileges of children and artists. To foster them is one of the most important tasks in the upbringing of a child. On the part of the parents, two things are presumed: (1) to understand or sense the needs of the child, and (2) to develop a certain sensitivity toward the things which surround us. The needs of the child change according to his age and development. A child of three has different needs than a child of ten has. But two ten-year-old youngsters may also develop differently, and therefore may have different needs. The needs which underlie the different age levels and developments will be discussed later under their respective headings.

Here we shall discuss only general experiences which lead to free growth and art expression. All art experiences are first perceived through our senses. Therefore, the sensitivity which we assist our children, from early childhood on, to develop for the things they see, hear, touch, or feel on their own bodies is of utmost significance. There are many people who go through the world without using the most precious gift we have received from God, the ability to see, touch, hear, and feel. These abilities were never cultivated in them, and they use them only for "technical" purposes, when they have to do it, and not from their own enjoyment. Today our increasingly rapid means of communication cut out many of these intimate personal experiences. Driving on a super highway at fast speeds makes use of the eyes only as a guide to direct the automobile. There is a great danger that those intimate relationships to the murmur of a brook, to the dew on the leaves, and to the precious "details" with which they are surrounded get lost. It is up to us parents to recapture sensitivity toward them wherever we find them. This is the most important task, and if we do not recognize it, we may succumb to our own technical achievements. We cannot start early enough in life. There are no limitations. Expose the baby to the lulling noise of a brook; make him conscious of it by saying, "Listen." Let him listen to the singing of a bird, the hushing of the wind through the trees. Make him aware of the brittle sounds of the fall foliage under your feet. Let him hold and touch whatever the opportunity offers. Open his eyes to whatever you are able to take in. One of my most precious memories is the moment in my childhood when I walked with my mother through the fields and saw the miracles of nature she made me see.

Whatever you can do to encourage your child in his sensitive use of his eyes, ears, fingers, and entire body will increase his reservoir of experience and thus help him in his art.

THE CORRECT MOTIVATION FOR MY CHILD'S CREATIVE WORK

We notice that there is a difference between what the child sees and what he expresses in his art. A five-year-old child may represent a man by only drawing his head and feet. This by no means indicates that a five-year-old child does not know more about a man. He knows perfectly well that a man has arms, hands, even fingernails. In his art work, however, he paints only what is important to him while he is painting. He may think, "My Daddy has a head and two big legs; my drawing has a head and two big legs"; therefore, "My drawing is Daddy." It is up to us to make Johnny's relationship to Daddy more sensitive by exposing him to some definite experiences with regard to Daddy. Daddy may lift him up, and Johnny will feel how Daddy's hands are holding him tightly. The next time he draws he will include Daddy's hands; they have become important to him.

Thus a good motivation consists in sensitizing some of the relationships which previously have remained passive or unused. Naturally, these relationships change, and we have to adjust our motivations to the needs of the growing child. However, the parent can never go wrong in exposing his child to experiences which make his ability to perceive more sensitive. Only when we start to impose upon the child experiences which are inconceivable to him, will we harm him.

Mary, who is seven, has no feeling for depth or distance in her painting. Neither depth nor distance is important to, or in her range of experience. She has not yet discovered this quality of her visual experience. It would not influence her at all to expose her to a widespread landscape through questions like, "Mary, how far can you see? Can you see the distant mountains?" Mary would never transfer such a motivation to her art expression. She is not ready for it. She can only take in the type of motivation and experiences which reach her level of development. It would, however, become very detrimental to her creative freedom if we were to tell her how the mountains appear smaller and smaller the more distant they are. It would be still worse if we insisted that she express depth and distance in her art work. This no longer would be a motivation, but an imposition. A good motivation should always leave to the child whatever she wants to express and how she chooses to do it.

Without any doubt the best motivation that the child can get at home is an atmosphere in which he feels secure and loved, in which sensitive relationships to objects and environment are encouraged not only when they are to be used for art expression, for life and art cannot well be separated. A child who grows up in such an environment will be continuously stimulated by her surroundings. Encouraged from the very beginning to use her eyes, her fingers, her senses of touch and hearing, as well as her feelings, she will react sensitively. Never becoming rigid in her reaction, she will change and remain flexibile toward the great variety of stimuli which she encounters.

The average American family, however, does not provide the child with these sensitive relationships which are so important in making children's lives rich and happy. We think too much in terms of jobs, money, and material goods. It is superfluous to say that material security is very important, but we know that material security alone does not make our life rich. Just as Virginia, surrounded by toys, will remain tense and unhappy unless she can use her imagination flexibily, so men with all their material wealth may not know how to live a happy life. The more this world becomes mechanized and materialized, the greater is our responsibility as parents to counterbalance this trend by emphasizing spiritual values. Needless to say, we create these values in our homes by exposing our children to experiences other than material ones. "Mary, look at this. Do you see those fine differences?" "Feel it, Mary, how velvety it is." "Listen to the sound of it." These are statements which should be constantly used everywhere. In such an environment, the child will not need any additional motivation for her art. Her art springs out of her daily experiences.

Unfortunately, many of our children have not grown up in such an environment. Some have become inhibited and need additional art motivations. The need of such motivations is seen whenever a child lacks confidence to express himself spontaneously, whenever a child says, "I can't draw."

WHAT CAN I DO WHEN MY CHILD SAYS "I CAN'T DRAW"?

A child who says "I can't draw" has become inhibited in the spontaneous creative expression of his experiences. We are often apt to believe that it may be an indication of lack of skill, that is, inability to represent things "adequately." That this is not so is borne out by the fact that children actually have no external standard for "adequate expression." Since all children express themselves differently according to their individual differences, there is actually no "right" or "wrong." If the child cannot express himself, something must have interfered with his self-confidence. Usually such interferences have three causes. The most common is adult interference through wrong criticism. The child was told his drawing did not look real, or was "not good enough," or he was shown "how to draw things." Since the child cannot do justice to such criticism, he escapes into the noncommittal attitude of "I can't draw." The second cause, frequently found, lies in the inability of the child to recall enough attributes of the objects which he intended to draw, or he may not have anything in mind at all. The third common cause is found in the fact that children have become conditioned to methods of copying or tracing, and once they have nothing to hold on to they feel incapable of producing something independently.

We shall deal with all three causes simultaneously, by assuming all three have interfered with the child's freedom of expression. Needless to say, we shall never again apply adult standards or criticism to children's art expression. We also shall abandon copybook methods.

If a child says, "I can't draw," we should never leave the child with such a generalization. "What is it that you would like to draw?" should be our next question. Just as a physician would not be satisfied with such a generalized statement of his patient as "I have pains," we are not satisfied with the generalization "I can't draw." Just as he tries to find out where your pains are, we try to find out what the child wanted to draw. Usually we get two kinds of answers. The child will either say, "Oh, I don't know—anything," or he will indicate a more or less generalized topic, such as, "I want to draw—a landscape," or, "I want to draw 'playing ball.'" "I don't know—anything," is an indication that the child has no experiences from which he can draw. It is up to us to provide him with experiences, or to draw them out of the child. "Johnny, I saw you yesterday when you helped Daddy fix our fence; let's find out what you did first. . . . Oh, you pounded the posts into the ground. How did you do that?" This is the first important step; you have made Johnny concentrate on a definite experience. He has to put himself in the place in which he was yesterday.

Let us see what happens to Johnny. Johnny's mind may have wandered around with nothing definite on which he could concentrate. Now he has been given something. Instead of aimlessly or nervously fluctuating in his mind, he now thinks of how he helped to pound the fence posts into the ground. As he recalls logically every step and action, he develops and trains his mind, his memory as well as his imagery. He thinks first of digging the hole, then of placing the fence post, and then, because he can't think of the next detail, he asks, "Mother, what did we use to pound the posts into the ground?" Now he recalls the heavy hammer; he thinks of it in detail. This continuous recall of detail will encourage him to look more closely next time. It will, in time, make him more sensitive toward the things he uses. The more a child has lost confidence in his own expression, the more he needs outside support for his establishment of sensitive relationships. Johnny will recall the texture of the surface of the fence post. He will remember the feeling he had when holding it. Questions such as, "Did you get a splinter in your hand?" will help to establish a vivid feeling toward his touch impressions. "Did it make a big bang when Daddy knocked the post into the ground?" may evoke a better atmosphere, for it includes "hearing." "Did you smell the wood when Daddy chipped it off?"

Now Johnny begins to paint. No longer is he without a topic, or only "neutral" to his topic. Now he knows what he wants to paint. He even recalls everything step by step. He may still interrupt and say, "Mother, I can't draw how Daddy knocks the post in."

This gives us an opportunity to consider the second case we mentioned, when a child says, "I can't draw 'playing ball' or 'Daddy knocking the post into the ground.' " This situation is by no means as difficult as the previous one. It merely indicates that the child cannot recall enough detail and needs some help in his ability to imagine. Our answer, therefore, should not relate to the child's drawing or painting but to his *experience*. We should not say, "You don't know how to draw 'playing ball' or 'Daddy knocking the post into the ground'?" We should refer to the experience by saying: "You don't know how to play ball? Let's find out how we play ball. Do you have your arms up or down when catching? Do you have a fist or your fingers stretched out?" Such a recall in *detail* will fortify the child's imagination and help him in his art expression. Johnny may even act out for us how Daddy knocked the posts into the ground. By doing so, he will feel like Daddy and learn *his* needs, an important educational function of art. If this is continually done, art motivations will help not only in establishing more sensitive relationships to our needs but also to the needs of others, "Daddy," and our neighbors in general.

If we deal with the third case, the child who has become conditioned to copying and tracing methods, the process of establishing confidence often becomes a most difficult one. If none of the foregoing methods is effective—and only if none is effective after *continuous* trial—the following is recommended. The child conditioned to depend on copying methods can only gradually be freed from it. In such instances it may be very helpful to start the child out with an experience which needs completion. Let us say that we recall with Virginia a party she has had. Remember that Virginia is tense and depends on given patterns. We draw a table with a few chairs on a piece of paper and ask Virginia to set the table for her party. Often clay is a better medium for such a purpose. We would then model a table or chairs, and ask Virginia to finish her party. At another time we watch a fire, a burning house. In this instance we could draw or paint the house, while Virginia could add the fire and the excitement connected with it. Gradually we employ smaller and smaller frameworks, until one day Virginia is able to start on her own. This would only be an indication of the fact that Virginia has gained sufficient self-confidence in her own experiences and no longer needs assistance from others. It would show that Virginia no longer depends on others' thought, and that she has become independent in developing her own. These are most important trends in the growth and development of her personality.

In conclusion, I should like to repeat that no specific art motivation is necessary for children who live in a home environment conducive to art expression, an environment in which a sensitive use of our senses is encouraged as a daily routine. Let us remember that it is much easier, and also more beautiful, when the art of our children grows naturally, hand in hand with their home life, than when tensions and difficulties arise which need special attention and which can only be removed with great effort.

WHAT MATERIALS SHALL I BUY?

While an abundance of materials may be diverting from the point of view of creative ability, it is necessary that the child be provided with the kind of art materials which will promote his art expression. Your child must never suffer in his art expression because of poor materials. This is just as discouraging to him as poor motivation. Just as a carpenter cannot build a cabinet with poor tools, a dull saw, and green wood, a child is greatly handicapped in his freedom of expression if he does not have the materials which fit his needs. Actually, there are different art materials which the child can better handle and appreciate during different stages in his development. A child of six years, for instance, may be greatly disturbed by the running and merging quality of water colors because he cannot utilize it in *his* art, while a ten-year-old child may be delighted by the same quality and experiment with it. Later, when the different age levels are discussed, a variety of art materials will be suggested which best agree with the respective levels.

Some general remarks, however, are given here because they apply to all levels. If you buy materials, don't save a few cents because you can get them more cheaply. There is nothing more valuable than your child's happiness and proper growth.

Crayons: When you buy crayons, buy the thick ones. Your child can hold them better and they don't break as easily. You can test the quality of your crayons by coloring a small area, putting pressure on the crayon. If you can scratch the wax off the paper with your fingernails, the crayons are not good. There is too much wax in the crayon and it is not well intermixed with the pigment. In good crayons pigment and wax are intimately combined, and the wax cannot be scraped off the paper. Crayons of good quality can easily be combined to form new colors by putting different layers of colors one on the other. Color an area with blue and put a layer of yellow over it. Is the result a good green? If not, your crayons are of poor quality. If thick crayons are not available in your community, buy the thin ones, but remember that they break easily. Some children will always like to keep their things as new-looking as possible. This tendency counteracts the free use of art materials. Many children are taught in schools to be "careful" with their materials, and some of them develop feelings of anxiety when their crayons break. I have seen children cry on such occasions. Others, who preserve the newness of their crayons and the boxes in which they come, proudly display them as a "sign of superior feelings," and thus discourage their co-workers in the free use of their materials. The easiest way in which such competition, harmful to the creative process, can be avoided is to break every crayon and put them on a tray after you have peeled off the paper. This has great advantages. The child, without hesitancy and fear that the crayon may break, can put as much pressure on it as he wants. There is no harmful competition between those who keep their crayons in "newer" condition and those who don't. By using only stumps of crayons, the child may be encouraged to experiment with the different uses of crayons, employing the broad side as well as the pointed end of the crayon. If you have more than one child, they can get along with one box. There is no need for buying boxes with a large selection of colors. On the contrary, the more "ready-made" colors you present to your child, the less will he use his imagination and creative urge to produce new colors by mixing. In general, boxes with few colors are sufficient to produce the rest by mixing, if the need for more colors arises. This need, however, depends on the age, development, and personality of the child.

Paper: When you buy *paper for crayons,* buy the regular newsprint (unprinted newspaper). If you cannot buy it where you live, your daily newspaper will gladly help you out. At the end of every roll there is a good deal of paper left which the printing machine cannot use. The newspaper will sell it to you very cheaply. But you may also get it in pad form. Don't buy small pads. They restrict your child. An 18″ x 24″ pad is just right. The child should have plenty of paper, and he should not be restricted in its use. We will see that the more our children develop the type of sensitivity conducive to art expression, the longer will they stay with one painting. The less they concentrate, the more they change to new sheets. However, it would be a misunderstanding to force children to stay with one work on the basis of too great a consumption of paper. They would only become bored with their work and would lose enjoyment and interest in creative activity. To have the child stay with one work cannot be artificially achieved by withdrawing the supply of paper.

Show-card paint: Another important material is *poster* or *show-card paint.* It can also be used satisfactorily with the newsprint we have described. Poster paint is on the market both in powder and liquid form. Each has specific advantages. The powder form of poster or tempera paint has the advantage that it can be mixed to any desired consistency. Since it is wiser to give young children thicker paint to prevent running, poster paint in powder form is preferable. In general, however, it has been found that the paint in powder form is not as bright and intensive as that in liquid form. It is more dull and chalky. Still, it is preferable for the younger child, while the liquid paint may be more stimulating for the older. Good poster paint should not be brittle and should not peel from the paper when it is dry. The child does not need more colors than yellow, red, blue, green, brown, black, and white. While green, brown, and black can be obtained through mixing, it is of advantage to include these colors. A cigar box may easily serve as a tray, with baby-food jars as containers. One large jar filled with water should always be ready for the cleaning of brushes. To keep the colors always in the same sequence makes mixing easier. No demonstration of *"how to use paint"* is necessary or even desirable. The child should find out for himself what can be done. To encourage this experimental attitude is part of the creative process.

The child should have good *brushes*. It is recommended that he have at least one flat bristle brush ¼" wide, one ½" wide, and one round hair brush No. 12. The hair brush when wet should have a well pointed end. All brushes should preferably have long handles.

Water colors: Some remarkably good qualities of water colors are on the market. Water colors should never be too dry and hard. Try to make an indentation with your fingernail. If the water color is too hard, it is not the type to buy for your child. Some water colors come in oval buttons. Your child will like them better than the square ones because he does not have to get into the corners and they are more suited to brush movements. In addition, small sets are preferred to large ones. They will encourage the child to mix his own colors and prevent him from using ready-made colors.

Paper for water color: A textured and nonabsorbent paper should be used. The paper which is on the market under the name of easel paper is very satisfactory. If the paper is too absorbent, the merging and flowing quality of water color cannot be explored as readily as when the paint does not penetrate the paper. This is of educational as well as technical significance. The more the child is encouraged in his experimental attitude through the material he is using, the greater the flexibility and freedom he will develop.

Clay or Plasticin: Too little attention is given in the home to the use of clay or plastic media. Many ideas can be carried out better in clay than in paint. If a child like Virginia has not developed enough confidence to express herself freely in painting, she may start to model with greater ease. In modeling she has the feeling that she can change her concept at all times because clay is pliable. If a painting does not turn out as she wanted it to be, she is discouraged. It cannot be changed like a modeling; it can only be destroyed. Clay can also be stored very easily. While previously the storage process of clay was a difficult one, especially at home, clay can now easily be stored in plastic bags obtainable in every better drugstore. In spite of this great advantage, clay has not yet become a popular art material. Virginia should not be restricted in the size of her modelings. If she has not enough clay, her modeling may be so small that she has difficulty in handling it. Have at least a five-pound bag of clay.

There are other plastic media on the market which serve the same purpose. Some plastics can be "fired" in an ordinary oven. For the very young child, the "firing" of clay or other materials may focus the child's attention too much on the final product. Such a diversion from the actual creative process may make the child overconscious of the final achievement. This would be harmful indeed for his growth and development. The older child, however, may enjoy seeing his finished product hardened and in final form.

Other materials: It is always good to have a pair of *scissors* ready for use. A set of *colored construction paper* is very stimulating for many creative projects. *Finger painting* is a medium which many children enjoy. We shall talk about its value elsewhere (page 81). A box of all kinds of *scrap material* is a very valuable addition to a creative workshop in the home. All kinds of items can be collected and occasionally used creatively: different kinds of string, wool, buttons, fiber, paper, fabric, woods, or other products of nature. All these may serve in time as good materials for creative products. They will be discussed elsewhere (pages 78 and 99).

WHAT SPACE AND EQUIPMENT SHOULD I PROVIDE

FOR MY CHILD'S ART ACTIVITIES?

The problem of space is most acute in early childhood. During the early years, especially when the creative impulses are strong and need release, the child has not yet developed a concept of what is socially "right" or "wrong." He may scribble on the walls of the living room or on the doors, to the great disgust of his parents. We must consider, however, that the more the child wants to scribble, the greater apparently is the force behind his wish and the greater is the necessity for an outlet. The more we restrict the child in these formative years, the more we harm him in his development. In fact, I strongly believe that we have no right to prohibit his scribbling on the walls unless we provide him with a space where he can freely release his creative energies. After all, human beings are more important than walls. This does not mean that we are in favor of leaving the walls to the child's scribbling. On the contrary, it means that we have to provide a space in our home upon which the child feels safe to scribble. If the problem continues, we can then insist that the child use the space which we have provided. In most cases, if the child has enough opportunity he will not need the walls.

The best place for the child is a corner with enough daylight, where he does not have to be too careful about his table or even the floor. A low and not large table with a washable linoleum top will be the best for his creative activity. The table should not be too large because he should be able to approach his work from different sides, and two persons should be able to work on one project when sitting opposite each other. The top of the table should be flat, not at an angle. Elaborate tables with tilting tops are neither necessary nor desirable. They produce an artificial "professional" atmosphere. I believe in the influence of simplicity. A stool is better than a chair with a back. In addition, the floor should be covered with linoleum.

A "Creative Corner" may become a fascinating problem in the furnishing of a home. The color of the linoleum square on the floor may be selected to harmonize with the color of the rest of the room, or even to oppose it. Linoleum may also be used on the walls, as a background for displays and at the same time as protection.

An easel may be a help for the older child, but it is by no means a necessity. The small child can paint much more easily on a level surface, where the danger of running paint is absent. Running paint only brings unnecessary discouragement.

The child should have some permanent space for his materials. The clay bag may hang on the wall. The paper should lie flat (not folded!) in a drawer or shelf always at his disposal. Another drawer or shelf should be provided for paint box, crayons, or poster paint, and a third drawer may be used for scrap treasure.

Much care should be taken to provide the child with proper light, natural as well as artificial. The child should never work in his own shadow.

In a good home the "Creative Corner" may become the place where the whole family can participate in creative experiences.

MY CHILD SEEMS VERY TALENTED TO ME

"My child is eight years old, and she is so gifted that she already uses perspective in her drawings. What should I do?" This is only one of the many questions which I encounter again and again. Another is: "My child draws so realistically, you would not believe it. Should I send her to an art school?" Almost all such questions which refer to "special talents" usually refer to attributes which appeal to adults. Thus, again we succumb to the imposition of our adult standards instead of considering child art on its own merits. Upon closer investigation of such claims, it has usually been found that in most of the so-called "gifted" cases "perspective" was taught, or methods of copying were used. Before we discriminate between specially gifted children and others who do not possess special talent, we should be clear about what we call a specially gifted child.

Needless to say, such a distinction is not significant if we promote creative art for *all* children. It is especially unimportant in the light of the fact that no prediction is possible for the development of special talent. Yet it would be a mistake to neglect the specially gifted, for we never know how far the child may develop.

That a child can copy well or imitate adult concepts does not mean he is specially talented. In fact, I have seen children possessing these special skills who were entirely lost when they were asked to produce creatively without a pattern to lean on. The special skills, in some instances, may even obstruct the child's creative development. This is especially true when parents, impressed by the skillful copying of their children, proudly point at it as a special achievement. By giving their children such encouragement, they promote skills but discourage independent thinking and creative attitudes.

We clearly have to distinguish between children who are especially gifted in creative art and those who, through their special skills, only appear to be gifted. Creatively gifted children are always independent and original in their concepts. In addition, they also possess the power to express them. Usually they express themselves with ease and have no doubts about their art expression. In addition, the art of gifted children does not necessarily have to be "pleasing" in terms of the common adult taste. Unfortunately, most often we do not recognize the really gifted child, because it is much more difficult to appreciate and understand *his* art than the "art" of the skillful imitator.

Needless to say, the talented child can succeed much more easily in his art expression without any particular motivation than can the less gifted or also the inhibited child. The problem of the parent of a gifted child is much more the one of not interfering with his gift by false criticism, or too much praise. What we have previously said about criticizing or praising the child (pages 19 and 20) is true for the gifted child to a much higher degree.

The most common notion among parents of gifted children is that a gifted child should go to an art school where he can learn techniques. The gifted child is still a child, and any imposition of adult standard is as harmful to him as to the average child. If there is no children's art class in town, do not send your child into an adult environment. Your child would soon become a poor "adult artist" and would lose all the freshness for which many adult artists envy him.

It is important, however, for your gifted child to have as much opportunity to experiment with as great a variety of art materials as he wants. Even oil painting may become a good creative medium for him.

The older the gifted child grows, the more important becomes the problem of preserving his special talent beyond his childhood. We shall, however, deal with this problem in a special section (page 175).

suggestions for parents
who have only one child

In creative activity the problem of having only one child is the same as in all other questions relating to the growth of the child. Much stimulation is obtained from a creative home atmosphere in which several children participate. When parents have only one child, they usually not only concentrate on his achievements, but also on his "apparent" mistakes. In other words, the single child gets too much attention. In addition, his creative expression is endangered by too much adult attention and influence. Too much attention only hinders the child in his development. In his expression he may easily become dependent on the accepted standard and after a time lose his spontaneous childish approach.

Parents who are aware of these dangers will welcome art as one of the most important means in the upbringing of only children.

In a house with more children many conflicts within the child are "worked out" of the child's system by play, fights, verbal means, and other forms of games which serve as an outlet for the child's tension or aggression. The single child who lacks these outlets must either find other means or, as often happens, become tense and unable to meet his problems. Art, then, has a double purpose: the purpose of substituting for the type of communication which naturally takes place in a larger family, and that of serving as a means of self-expression. The child in a larger family may have had some disturbing experiences. He gets rid of his tension by starting a fight with his brother. It is much more difficult for the single child. Whatever bothers him can only be settled in himself or by behavior which is quickly criticized and subdued by his parents. If he has his art, he can use it as his "younger brother," tell it stories, fight with it, and after a hard battle feel relieved again. Art, then, becomes a natural means of balance in the life of the single child whose emotional and social problems are much more centered upon himself than are those of the child who can work them out with his brothers and sisters.

However, when your child becomes nine or ten years old, and the desire for associating with other children becomes acute, the child should have group experiences in art also. Usually, the schools take care of this. We shall speak about "creative afternoons in our homes" in the section that deals with respective age levels.

suggestions for parents
who have more than one child

THE problem of giving one child more attention than another and the resulting complications and jealousies from such preferences are widely known in the upbringing of children.

The seriousness of such problems as they are affected by art may be best illustrated by a case of a brother and a sister reported in greater detail elsewhere.* "The girl was very gifted, the boy average. The girl was always the favorite in the family; the boy was neglected. The girl painted very well. The boy, who could not paint as well as his sister, began to imitate her by taking over the same kind of representation his sister used in her paintings. He hoped thus to gain the attention of his parents, just as his sister got it with the same means. The boy became more and more involved with a kind of representation that was not at all in accord with his own experience. It was as though he was trying to

* Viktor Lowenfeld, *Creative and Mental Growth*, rev. ed. (New York, The Macmillan Company, 1952), p. 3.

speak a language that he was not able to understand. Whereas his sister was happy in creating new forms and thoughts, his anxiety to copy his sister prevented him from living his own life. Therefore the child grew more and more sick mentally as well as emotionally. When he came home, he would throw himself on his bed and cry for no obvious reason—at least his mother could not discover the reason—and the child became extremely introverted and withdrawn."

On my suggestion the parents encouraged the child in his own creative activity. This was easily done by *changing the medium*. They gave him clay, which he had not used previously, and the change promoted the boy's return to his own kind of expression. Since his sister mainly painted, he felt important in his own manner of modeling, which, on my suggestion, the parents now appreciated in the same way as they did the paintings of his sister. Having found self-confidence in his own creations, the child grew happier, lost all signs of disturbance, and was quite changed. The parents, very happy at this result (which required about seven months to achieve), learned the correct way of showing their appreciation for both children.

We have seen from this case that through the efforts the child made to get attention by imitating his sister's paintings, he grew more and more tense and fixed on a kind of representation which was not the expression of his own experiences. Fixation on his sister's expression finally halted the whole mental development of the child. Therefore, never prefer one child's creative work over that of another! Each child's creative work is equally important and stands on its *own* merits. Never set the work of one child as an example to another!

If each child knows that he can succeed in expressing himself with his own means, art can become a family occasion, an ideal democracy, in which all can participate, including the parents, as individuals. It is, however, most important that parents keep in mind the maintenance of a proper balance in their appreciation of their children's works. "Johnny, tell me about your painting. Oh, I like the way you are throwing the ball in your picture." "What did you do, Mary? Oh, I love the way you painted your dress." None of the works need to be pleasing to the adult's eye. If they express the child's needs, they have fulfilled their highest purpose.

As children get older and ready for group work, "Creative Afternoons" to which other children can be invited will further cooperation in the family and outside. We shall read about them in another section (page 136). It may, however, be pointed out that children of various age levels can successfully work together, as long as the final product is not emphasized. *To develop a feeling of tolerance* is one of the important outcomes of good group and family atmosphere. This feeling for tolerance cannot be encouraged early enough. It is first promoted by the parents' proper recognition of individual differences in the styles and art concepts of their children. "Johnny, I like the house in your painting very much. I also like it because it is so different from Mary's." Sometimes the children, through their own criticism, may offer good opportunities for stressing tolerance. If Johnny does not like Mary's clouds, we can explain to Johnny: "Mary has the right to make her cloud as she wants it, and you, Johnny, can make it as you want. I love to see different clouds." Such attitudes are very important since they create tolerance not only within the family but outside it.

can I work creatively with my child?

THE question, "Are children influenced by adult standards if they work in their presence?" may occur. Experiments have proved that this depends entirely on the adult who works creatively in the presence of his child. There are children of artists who work in the presence of their parents and produce entirely unhampered child art, and there are children of artists who are handicapped because they want to do what Daddy or Mother produces.

Just as children of different age levels can work happily, respecting each other's way of expression, so can parents participate without influencing their children's concepts. Great care, however, is necessary, especially at the beginning. If the children are not conscious of the final product, and do not compare their works with others it is easy to establish a good creative atmosphere, for the very fact that several people are concerned with the same activity produces a wholesome atmosphere. If a child says that he does not know what to paint, the parent should start him off with a little stimulation or a story. "Johnny, when you were skating down the hill, how did you feel?" Sometimes, just for a change, it may be wise to tell a story from which children can select the part which impressed them most. In telling a story, frequent interruptions, asking the child to place himself in the story, are very helpful in creating an atmosphere conducive for creative expression. Only when the story has become *the child's own experience* will he be able to use it creatively. "Mary, imagine how you would feel if you were all by yourself in the woods, with Johnny, just like Hänsel and Gretel, with no one else around. What would you hear? Just the breaking twigs under your feet, a few birds singing, perhaps a barking dog far in the distance—what else?" Such interruptions encourage children to identify themselves with the story until they feel they are a part of it.

This is very important not only for their creative work but also for their attitudes in general. Without such close participation we will not be happy in our work, whatever we are doing. Our world greatly suffers from the inability of people to see purpose and meaning in their work. To do work only for the purpose of making one's living will contribute neither to the quality of the work nor to one's own happiness. The mechanical age in which we are living by no means promotes the attitude of close participation. In mass production it becomes increasingly difficult to see purpose and meaning in the things we are doing. Try to make a chair, from the beginning to the finished product, so that you can see and control its purpose and meaning both aesthetically as well as functionally. You become absorbed in your work whether you want to or not. To see meaning and purpose in a detail, where you scarcely know the whole, as in modern mass production, is very difficult indeed. You can easily become absorbed in a "hobby" of your own choosing. But how beautiful it is when your job becomes your hobby!

Our world suffers also from our inability to put ourselves into the place of others, as Mary put herself into the place of Gretel and Johnny into that of Hänsel. The basic assumption for any cooperative attitude is the ability to put one's self into the place of another. How can we learn of the needs of others if we are only thinking of ourselves?

If we continuously stress this close participation of each child in the story which we are telling, we shall promote not only a creative atmosphere but also a most important attitude for the future of our children and the world.

However, if children are very conscious of their final products, the parent can easily capitalize on this by saying: "We all would feel different in the woods. Let's find out how *different* our paintings will be." Such an attitude, when continuously stressed, may gradually divert a child's attitude from the significance of the final product to the significance of individual differences, the backbone of our democracy.

There is another very important meaning in the participation of parents and children in creative activities. I believe that there is no better opportunity for parents to learn to know their children than through their creative work and their spontaneous reactions while they produce. Many things which parents would never find out easily reveal themselves during the creative process. The reason for this is quite obvious. Many tensions and experiences and restrictions which are present in the child but are somewhat buried do not express themselves because the child is not relaxed enough to freely "dispose" of them. During the creative process the child concentrates on what he produces by putting himself into its place. It has been experimentally proven that this concentration on the creative process produces a spontaneous atmosphere in which the child reveals himself without the usual restrictions and controls. I have heard children continuously talk, during the process of creating, about things which they never would be able to reveal spontaneously without the creative stimulus. I have also heard children suddenly cry out things which are very important and revealing for them. Recently a child, while he was drawing the attic of his house, said: "I know why I must never go into the attic. There is a secret there." When asked what it was, he said, "My first daddy is hidden there." His father had been killed during the war, and he had somehow developed the idea that he was hidden in the attic. When his mother was told about it, she went up to the attic with the child, showed him around, and thus probably prevented a serious obsession from developing any further. The mother had had no idea that the precautionary measure of not allowing her child to climb the steep ladder to the attic had created such suspicion in him. She might never have found it out by different means.

I dare say that our world would be quite different if parents would set aside weekly "Creative Afternoons" for themselves and their children. Their children would grow up to respect individual differences in others, and they would develop early the attitude of close participation in their own work and identification with the needs of others. Above all, parents would learn more about themselves, their children, and their relationships to them.

*when should children begin
to draw or paint?*

THERE is actually no limitation as to when children should begin to draw or to paint. The child begins to express himself verbally as soon as he starts to babble. We know that some infants babble sooner than others, and it is of no particular significance for their later life whether they start somewhat sooner or later. While children would as naturally begin to draw or paint as they begin to babble, there is one decisive difference. For his babbling the child is continually motivated by the conversation of people around him. How much "listening" contributes to the child's developing language can be seen in the difficulty which deaf children have in developing language. Since there is no stimulus around the child which produces motivation for drawing or painting as natural and adequate as the one of speaking people, we have to play a more active part in the promotion of art activities.

Needless to say, it is here where the greatest harm can be done. Parents in general realize that they should do something "to make their children draw." But what they usually do is to buy coloring books. This confronts children from the start with patterns inconceivable to them. Just as we would not impose the correct pronunciation of words on a babbling infant, we should not confront the child with inconceivable pictures. Usually the child completely disregards the pictures in coloring books and scribbles all over them. This is, however, no excuse for giving coloring books to children, for it will become a devastating habit once we have started to buy them. Since we have thoroughly discussed the effect of them on pages 12 to 16, this should be only a reminder.

How far, then, can we go in playing a more active part in the promotion of art activities? Our natural positive and appreciative reaction when the child himself starts should be enough in a normal situation. In addition, we should provide the child with proper art materials (see pages 31 to 35). From then on the child takes over, and it depends upon him as to whether he needs continuous encouragement or develops his stimulation out of his own work. It should be kept in mind that, as in other activities, such as reading and writing, the child's readiness and desire to perform the task determines his progress. Forcing will only have a detrimental effect.

shall I encourage my child to participate in contests?

FROM our previous discussion we have seen that the important part in art activities is the influence which the creative process has on our children and not the final product. How far contests and competitions do justice to this all-important contribution of art to the child's growth needs thorough discussion.

Competition actually is a part of our daily living; it goes on everywhere in every healthy society, stimulated by the drive for "more" and "better." One of the most important forms of competition is the competition which takes place in ourselves. Johnny wants to find out whether he can do better than he has done before. Actually, growth is a continuous competition with one's own standards and achievements. It is the most natural form of competition. Competition also is a very healthy part of every family situation as long as each individual can compete by means of his own standards. Not only Mary, but Johnny also wants to express the trip to the zoo. Johnny, in expressing *his* impression of the zoo, will not compare his creative work with that of Mary because Mary painted *her* impression. Both impressions were different, but Johnny, seeing that Mary had started, wanted to go ahead too.

There is, however, another form of competition which is usually called a "contest." In a contest a certain standard must be met, and prizes are given as stimulus and reward. Such contests are very common, and are usually known to parents from the school work of their children. Parents know best how much discouragement has resulted through the participation of their children in such contests. A child of eight years who won a high award in a recent contest could not even recognize his own drawing. This is by no means rare. Children quickly change and grow, and therefore lose contact with their former expression. But the other children in the classroom were very jealous, and lost interest in their work, particularly the ambitious ones. Another child, in another school, also won a prize, but he did not know why he had won, nor did the other children in the classroom. However, since the child who won the prize drew his animal with the flat part of his crayon, *all* children in the classroom drew with the flat part of the crayon from then on. Thus the contest not only directed the children's attention to the final product but stimulated them to imitate. In this way they lost confidence in their own ability to express themselves. The child has no understanding of why somebody else's drawing won a prize. For him there are no "rights" or "wrongs" in creative expression. If "standards" are imposed upon him, they will harm his personality because they suppress his individual differences.

Since the child does not use "techniques" consciously, an emphasis on the final product may make him conscious of techniques, and thus take away his spontaneous approach.

Very often a child expresses experiences in his creative products which are not understandable even to the experienced juror, yet they may be highly significant for the child and his development. In contests, usually those creative works which are beautiful to the adult's eye or those which are "original" receive awards. "Original," however, usually means outwardly different. Those children, and they may be yours, who express themselves sincerely, but neither "originally" nor especially "beautifully," never have a chance of receiving awards in contests. Yet they might be the children who most urgently need creative activities because for them the freeing of their personalities is most important. No artificial stimulation, no matter how high the reward may be, can replace the sound experience which is necessary in any creative work.

There is another aspect to contests, especially when they are conducted in schools. This is the time-consuming effort of preparing for them, and the pressure on children to meet a deadline. I have seen schools which are constantly geared to work for contests. Instead of being proud when one's own child is the happy winner of a prize, while many others are the remaining frustrated ones, parents should awaken to the harmful and devastating influence which art contests have on the personalities of their children.

shall I send my child to art classes?

WITHOUT any doubt, working in a group is an important experience for a child, especially an only child. Recently a parent brought her child to our children's art classes with the remark that her son, who is eight, never draws or even touches crayons. She looked rather worried about it, and added, "You'll have a hard time with him." After the first art class was over, her son participated in all activities like every other child, happily creating in his own way. Children behave differently in groups than at home. It might also happen that the mother, in spite of her best intentions, did not have the right approach to her child (Fig. 5).

Art classes are certainly a blessing for children when they are well conducted, that is, when children have the freedom to express themselves according to their own personality. But don't send your children to art classes as you would mail a parcel, being happy that it arrives at its destination on time. Try to get all advantages from the art classes for your home life and for the growth of your child.

Art classes, and we speak here of art classes outside the school, have become a wonderful American institution. They can be found everywhere, in museums, community centers, churches, and schools. Be sure that when you send your child to an art class it is a *children's* art class. Make sure also that it serves no other purpose but the one of helping your child to express himself.

5 In children's art classes children are encouraged to express themselves individually. They also learn to cooperate. (See page 52) Courtesy Chicago Public Schools.

There you can get much valuable information about your child which otherwise you would not be able to obtain—how your child behaves in a group, whether his reactions are different from those when he is at home, whether he talks much while he creates, or whether he keeps everything to himself, and much other interesting information. Please don't expect "beautiful" paintings from your child, because they are the exception in an art class. Remember that what we have said of your child's art and its influence on his growth and personality is true for the home as well as for the art class. If you feel that the teacher at the art class tries to do things with which you do not seem to be in agreement, don't develop hostile attitudes or withdraw your child from the art class. It is always best to talk things over, and in most instances you will find your art teacher cooperative and happy when she can find someone who is interested in the art of her child (Fig. 5).

some do's and don't's for parents

DO'S	DON'T'S
Do regard the child's art as a record of his personality.	Don't "correct" or "help" the child in his work by imposing your personality.
Do realize that during the time the child works, he acquires important experiences for his growth.	Don't regard the final product as significant.
Do make the child sensitive in his relationship to his environment.	Don't expose the child to coloring books or patterns which make him insensitive.
Do appreciate it if the child has succeeded in expressing his experience.	Don't appreciate the child's work indiscriminately.
Do realize that "wrong" proportions most often express an experience.	Don't correct wrong proportions.
Do learn that your child's feeling toward his art is different from yours.	Don't expect your child's art always to be pleasing.

DO'S

DON'T'S

Do appreciate your children's art on its own merit.

Don't prefer one child's work to that of another.

Do provide your child with some space where he can work.

Don't restrict your child's work by not giving him the proper working space.

Do encourage your children to respect one another's expression.

Don't compare your children's art.

Do encourage the type of competition which grows out of the child's urge to express himself.

Don't encourage contests which use prizes and rewards as stimulation.

If you work with your child creatively, do encourage tolerance and respect for each other's work.

Don't impose your standard upon the child's standard when you work with him.

Do send your child to art classes.

Don't keep your child all to yourself.

Do hang your children's art work on the wall only when all children can participate, and not only through one work.

Don't hang only the "best" example of your child's art on the wall.

Do let the child develop his own technique by experimentation.

Don't show the child "how to paint."

some general problems for all age levels

MY CHILD NEVER TALKS ABOUT HIS ART

THERE are children who think only in terms of pictures and not in terms of words. They have a rich imagination but may have a poor vocabulary. They may feel free to express themselves on paper but may be restricted when communicating with others. Virginia always sits at home and paints, but she has difficulty with her English.

A child who feels restricted in her verbal expression apparently has lost confidence in it. Since Virginia feels that she cannot freely communicate with others verbally, she tries to give expression to her feelings in other ways. Painting has become a major outlet for her. Yet it would be wrong to leave her alone with her paintings. If the child lacks verbal expression, her paintings should be used as a stimulus for her language expression: "Virginia, tell me about your painting." If Virginia still does not want to talk, be more particular in your questions. "What is this in your painting? What does this mean? What is the girl doing in your picture?" If we make it a habit to ask Virginia to talk about her

56

paintings, she gradually may grow out of her verbal restriction and get used to talking.

MY CHILD TALKS MUCH ABOUT THINGS
WHICH ARE NOT IN HIS PAINTING

Apparently your child's talking about things which are not in his painting reveals that he can talk more easily than he can paint. Words come to him quicker than thinking in terms of pictures. When he sits down and paints, he cannot think of how things look, nor concentrate long enough on his paintings. Yet, in talking, many things come out which we would never know through his paintings. He thinks in words and not in pictures. His imagery (the thinking in terms of pictures) apparently is not sufficiently developed. This is unfortunate because the words he uses would be so much more meaningful if they were backed by images, if he also could visualize what he says. For Johnny, it would then be very important to develop his imagination and counterbalance

6 My child talks much about things which are not in his painting.

his verbal expression. If Johnny tells about things which we cannot see in his paintings, there is nothing wrong with stopping him and asking him to what he refers. "Johnny, you spoke of a storm blowing the leaves from the tree, but there is no storm in your picture and I can't see the leaves blown from the tree. Next time when you paint, you tell yourself the story and paint *everything* you can think of." If he has difficulty or will not react to this, you may ask him to write his story down and then paint it. This may give him a better chance to concentrate on each item, step by step. While his creative work may appear somewhat forced in the beginning, it may gradually develop a greater balance in his personality and lead to a freer art expression (Fig. 6).

MY CHILD ALWAYS DRAWS THE SAME THING (AIRPLANES, HORSES, TRAINS, FASHION FIGURES, ETC.)

If your child continually draws the same thing, there may be two reasons for this. Your child may either be specifically interested in the one item, or his mind may not be flexible enough to invent, explore, and imagine other things. Since this is of great importance for his proper guidance, I shall try to explain the two reasons in greater detail (Fig. 7a).

Be sure that you differentiate between the two reasons because one means that your child is mentally alert, but may be too much interested in one thing, while the other means that your child is emotionally not as free as he should be. You can distinguish the two reasons very easily. If your child is particularly interested, let us say in airplanes, he will draw different kinds of airplanes in different situations, diving, landing, going up, and so on. He will also draw them in different views. If your child, however, has developed a certain emotional inflexibility, he will draw the same airplane over and over again. Such repetitions of the same thing, whether it is an airplane, a figure, or anything else, indicate that the individual cannot adjust to a new situation easily. For instance, whenever Virginia sits down and begins to paint, her mind is fixed on one thing—the figure which she keeps repeating. This repetition, however, gives her a certain security. She knows she can draw the figure again and again. She also knows that she does not need to meet new situations when she draws. It is for her a certain escape pattern into which she withdraws whenever she cannot do justice to a situation. It

7a   My child always draws the same thing.   (See page 58)

7b   My child always draws airplanes.   (See page 60)

is the same reaction that you find when children who cannot follow an order, that is, adjust to a given situation, escape into a tantrum. A tantrum is also an emotional pattern, a repeated reaction which is used whenever the child cannot adjust to a given situation. If Virginia draws the same figure again and again in the same way, Virginia definitely needs some help. The degree to which she is fixed at one representation will indicate the kind of help she needs. You as a parent have the best possibility of seeing how these characteristics in her drawings correspond with the rest of her behavior.

Let us find out what we can do to make Johnny's interest broader and to alleviate Virginia's emotional conditions.

Johnny is interested in airplanes only. Such an interest, when developed too early in life and over too long a period of time, may prevent his getting a broader interest in life in general. He may become one-sided too early, when "specialization" is not a scientific urge but a romantic idea. It may prevent him from participating in many things which he later will miss. To broaden his interest should not be difficult if we follow the general rule not to break a habit but to try to put ourselves in Johnny's place. If we do that, we shall immediately understand that breaking his interest would only cause frustration or bad reactions in him. If you love something you don't want to part with it. However, it is possible gradually to develop a broader interest by starting with *his* specialty. We always start on the child's level. It is up to you to take first a specific interest in airplanes. Only if your interest is a sincere one will you gain Johnny's confidence. If you have achieved this first step, you can begin with the process of gradually broadening his interest. Never ridicule his interest. Don't say, "You always draw nothing but these silly airplanes," as I have often heard it said. See Fig. 7b. Don't be authoritative either: "No airplanes any more!" Such remarks would not only cause frustration to the child, but would certainly boomerang against your own intentions. Education is a gradual process. Johnny's interests are strongly tied up with airplanes. You should be glad that your child has developed some kind of interest, and should capitalize on it. Your motivations to broaden his interest depend on the child. If Johnny draws only one kind of plane, let us say military planes, you may want to interest him in civilian planes of different kinds and sizes. Remember that your intention is not to improve Johnny's skill in art, but to make his mind more flexible so that he will become interested in things other than airplanes. "Airplanes fly over different kinds of country. Johnny, I'd like to see over which kind of country your plane is flying. How would it be if we were to fly over the North Pole and run out of gas? Let's paint what we would do!" Of course, there are innumerable stories to be invented to catch Johnny's feelings and understanding and pull him away from the narrow scope of his former interest.

Needless to say, the same technique can be applied to any other "narrow" interest. If Mary, at a certain age, starts to draw fashion-magazine figures, you should endeavor to enlist her interest in the variety of fashions, in the many occasions at which different dresses are worn. "How would we dress if we went on a hike, in winter, in summer? Or let's go to a picnic." Here your aim is to broaden Mary's mind by making her accept other than fashion figures. We will not have much difficulty with Mary, especially if Mary feels that we have a sincere interest in the things in which she is interested.

It may not be so easy to alleviate Virginia's emotional conditions. But we can only help her and not harm her, so let us try it.

Before all, we must understand Virginia. Virginia is not intentionally tense, nor is she responsible for her emotional reactions. Because she may suffer from them as much or more than the people around her, let us approach her with love, sympathy, and a feeling of interest in her. She may need this more than anything else. Apparently Virginia was not strong enough to withstand all the influences and experiences to which she has been exposed. She has built up a world around her, a world of her own, and surrounded herself with a protective wall. Because she does not want new experiences to reach her, she draws the same thing again and again, the same figure—without change. Any change is disturbing for her because change means adjustment. To some people changes are exciting; they look forward to changes, especially pleasant ones. But what is pleasant for one may be upsetting for another, like traveling or moving to another place. It all depends on the flexibility of individuals to adjust to new situations. For Virginia, even small changes are upsetting, like giving her an order. She was not expecting an order; she could not adjust quickly enough to it; and it upset her. She gets upset easily because she never has time enough to adjust. Let's try to approach Virginia more gradually. First of all, we ought not to confuse her by asking her for several things at the same time. Perhaps if we find out her state of mind first, approach her gently, and try to help her to adjust gradually to a new situation—an order, or whatever it may be—it will help her.

This is exactly what we try to accomplish through our art motivations. We try to start again with her experience on the level of her comprehension. She may have filled a page with figures which are all alike, as in Fig. 7a. For her, these were not a number of different girls; they were merely a process of adding one figure to another, without any particular intention, like doodling. The first step may then well be to make Virginia conscious of the fact that these are different girls. "Virginia, what a nice group of girls you have here. They are all alike, aren't they?" This would make her immediately conscious of her present state, which is our point of departure. Of course, our aim remains always to help Virginia in her apparent adjustment difficulty. Any change from rigid repetition would then indicate that Virginia could put herself into the place of her figures at least to some extent. The kind of change which we intend to motivate depends, of course, on Virginia and her special likings. For instance, if Virginia loves dresses, we could say: "One girl just got a new dress." "Which one is it?" If Virginia is conscious of movements, we could start a story of what happened when Virginia fell and hurt her knee. "Which one of the girls fell and hurt her knee? Where did she fall? Was the ground covered with gravel or grass?" Such questions, applied after some time, may introduce a feeling for environment. This feeling is most important since it will permit her to adjust her mind to her surroundings. Such continuous adjustments in her creative work merely indicate her greater flexibility.

Another method, which has been discussed previously, may also be of help to Virginia—the shift to another material. To give her clay may be enough of a change for Virginia so that she will discontinue her rigid repetitions. Clay has the advantage that she can change her concept at all times as long as the clay is pliable. Even if she were to start to make all figures alike, we could say, "Let's all sit around a campfire." Then she could merely bend her clay figures to the sitting position and place them around a prepared "campfire." The bending, that is, the adjustment from a standing to a sitting figure, already presumes some flexibility on her part.

The more Virginia develops her flexibility, the more she becomes aware of the meaningfulness of art to her. With her greater range of experiences the desire to express herself develops. This is also true of language expression. The more words there are at your disposal, the better you express yourself and the more urge you develop to use your words. But let us remember that perfection also develops from the urge for expression.

MY CHILD PAINTS "SLOPPILY"

Depending on their own background, "sloppy" has a different meaning for different people. In countless cases I could detect the parent's desire for neatness in the paintings of children. This is particularly true for parents whose occupations demand exactness. Parents must be careful not to restrict the child's freedom of expression by imposing their own concepts of neatness.

In child art "sloppy" may refer to what is expressed in a picture as well as to how a painting looks. In most instances we usually refer to sloppy paintings with regard to their looks, their outward appearance. The child splashes paint on places "where it does not belong"; he paints outside the boundaries; his brush strokes seem to be uncontrolled (Figs. 8 and 9).

It is important to remember that whatever the child does is an expression of his personality! Thus, if we would "make him" paint neatly, it would only affect his painting, but not his personality. It would again mean curing a rash, caused by an upset stomach, by means of an ointment. In both instances we would be using an artificial "cure" without getting at the cause of the symptom.

If a child expresses himself carelessly or sloppily, there may be two causes. One is purely physical; the child's coordination is disturbed or his vision is impaired. This implies that the child is physically unable to control his motions or that he cannot see accurately enough. In doubtful cases, only a physician may determine the right answer. The other cause apparently is owing to the child's lack of desire to be more neat or precise with his art. The reason for this may be part of the child's reaction toward his environment, or lack of interest in his work. If a child discovers that people cannot understand him because his language poorly expresses what he means, he will, according to the importance of his message, try to express himself. The more important it is to him that people understand him, the harder he will try. As we have previously said, perfection grows with the urge for expression. Every parent knows that at one point or another their son or daughter gets a compulsion to whittle a bow, to make a special sling shot, or to sew a special dress for a special occasion. I have seen boys develop an unbelievable degree of perfection in making sling shots. They did not stop making them until they had produced one of high quality.

8   My child paints sloppily.   (See page 63)   Courtesy of Keith School, Indiana, Pa.

If the same urge can also be produced for art expression, Johnny no longer would paint outside an area which is highly important to him. In fact, Johnny would be greatly disturbed by the fact that he did not remain within the area.

If a parent feels that her child does not paint neatly enough, she would only cause a greater tension in the child and less creative urge if she were to tell him to paint more neatly. Such an order remains an imposition as long as the desire for less sloppiness does not come from the child. The only way we can succeed in creating this desire is to make art expression an important part of the child's development.

9 My child draws sloppily. (See page 63)

Parents have asked me whether children cannot learn to remain within lines by means of the exercises that exist in coloring books. The effect of filling in pictures which were not created by the child but by some adult has been discussed on page 12. Obviously the child does not connect any urge to express something important to him with these pictures. Therefore there is no voluntary urge to remain within the lines on the part of the child, except the external one of completing a picture to which one has little or no connection. In fact, experiments have shown that children much more frequently remain within the boundaries they create in their own pictures than in those in coloring books.

Self-discipline, the discipline which grows out of the child's *own* desire for expression, is much more vital for growth than the restricting, imposed discipline of coloring books which is derived from outside forces.

MY CHILD DOES NOT KNOW WHAT TO DRAW OR PAINT

It has been said before that basic to art expression is the fact that it comes from a definite experience. The greater the intensity of the experience, the more it lends itself to creative expression. If your child does not know what to draw, it may be because of two reasons. Either he may not be able to make up his mind which topic he wants, or he may not have any experiences which are intensive and tangible enough for him to use. In both instances we can help him.

First, we must discover which of the two causes bothered him. Therefore we ask Johnny whether he has something on his mind. If he says, "Yes, but I don't know what to paint," we must inquire in greater detail. "What are the thoughts you have on your mind?" may lead to a good start. If we want to help Johnny to make up his mind, we must know that some topics are better than others for creative expression. Topics which are mere descriptions, with no feelings or other experiences involved, are not good. Johnny may say: "I don't know what I should draw; an airplane or our campfire." There is no question about it; a campfire involves much more individual participation. It offers a great range of possibilities to include what he sees and what he feels in himself and toward others. Therefore we ask him specific questions about the campfire. "Johnny, where was the campfire? Did you say it was near Spring Creek? Was it late in the evening? Was it a warm day? How many people were there? Did you collect wood? Did you sing camp songs?" Such questions will focus Johnny's attention on the campfire, and soon you will start him painting it.

However, what are we to do if Johnny did not give us such a clear-cut choice, where one topic offered more involvement of his own experiences. When Johnny, for instance, says, "I don't know what I should draw; an airplane or a locomotive," the problem becomes more complicated. In this instance it is important to find out whether Johnny has more "personal relations" to a plane or to a locomotive. "Johnny, how does it feel riding on a locomotive? Do you think it is hot where the engineer stands? Do you think of a locomotive with a lot of power?

What kind of locomotive did you think of?" If Johnny says, "Oh, I don't know," or gives another evasive answer, you may be sure that he did not connect any definite experience to a locomotive, and you may switch to the airplane with similar questions. However, if Johnny insists, and says, "I just want to draw a locomotive," then he apparently has in his mind to draw a technical representation. This we should not call art expression. In any creative expression, the individual is a part of it, with his thinking, feeling, and perceiving.

If Johnny, however, does not know what to paint or draw because his experiences are not intensive and tangible enough, then he needs to be stimulated in his sensitive relationships to experiences. Any more detailed reference to experiences, as indicated under "The correct motivation for my child's creative work" (page 27), will then be helpful. As has been said in this section, specific motivations differ in regard to the age levels and developmental stages of your child. In what follows, we shall deal with questions as they refer to these different levels.

the scribbling child: the 2-4 year old

ONE of the first means with which the child expresses himself is movement. Every parent has seen the child in the cradle moving his arms and kicking with his legs while he is babbling or crying; but not only the movements in which the baby actively engages are affecting him. Every parent also knows the calming effect of picking up and rocking her crying baby or even simply rocking his cradle. The significance of body movements as one of the first sources of expression and communication has been pointed out by many psychologists.

When the child is about two (some children earlier, others later), he will, when he gets hold of a crayon, start to make marks on the paper. In the beginning these motions appear to be uncontrolled (Fig. 11). The child simply enjoys them. We need only to watch Mary to see how absorbed she is while she scribbles. Indeed, scribbling is very important to her, and we should not disturb her or interrupt her. We must not deprive her of such an important release.

At some point, perhaps six months after she has started scribbling, Mary will discover that she can produce motions on the paper of her

10   My child only scribbles.

own free will. She finds out that she can even control them. This gives
her much satisfaction, and she does it over and over again. This we
can see in her repeated motions on the paper. The experience of guiding and controlling her motions on the paper gives her confidence. It
is a first experience. We can only understand the importance of it if
we consider that most of our activities are based on the apparently

simple coordination of body movements such as walking, almost all manual skills, speech, and many others. This is very important to know because only with this in mind will we understand how much harm we would do to our child if we were to interfere with her scribbling by imposing tasks on her which she can neither understand nor perform.

11   My child scribbles without control.   (See page 68)

As Mary assures herself that she can master her motions by repeating them, she tries the same thing in other situations, as in eating, where she also discovers that she *can* guide her spoon from the cereal to her mouth. It is senseless to force a child to eat properly at a time when the coordination and control of motions is still inconceivable to her. Yet how often do we see parents who scold their little children because they smear the cereal all over their mouths. A child who cannot conceive of controlling his motions cannot be made responsible for improper eating any more than a babbling child can be made responsible for articulating and pronouncing words incorrectly. Mary will learn to eat properly much more easily, quicker, and without frustration when you have discovered that her lines in her scribblings are repeated and controlled. (See Fig. 12.)

12   My child controls her motions.   (See page 70)

13   My child scribbles in little jerks.   (See page 72)

WHAT DOES SCRIBBLING MEAN TO MY CHILD?

Scribbling to your child means enjoyment, happiness, release, and the gaining of a most important function, the coordination of motions.

To understand the real significance of scribbling we have to try hard to put ourselves in the place of our child. The younger a child, the fewer are his emotional outlets and means of expression. A baby can only cry or kick his arms and legs as an expression for his discomfort. He has no other means of communication. Even if Mary is two or three years old, and something happens to her, she has no possibility of rationalizing. For instance, if she gets an injection at the physician's, she sees and feels only what is done to her. The "why" does not even enter her mind. Since there are many things which just "happen" to her and with which she has to cope with her very limited means, every form of expression which helps to release tension is extremely important.

MY CHILD SCRIBBLES IN LITTLE JERKS

When your child is absorbed in his scribblings, he has no time to look around or even to interrupt his motions. It is usually a sign of lack of confidence and concentration if children frequently interrupt their scribbling. The child who is not afraid, and who is experimental in attitude, scribbles in determined motions.

If a child has become restricted in his motions by external or other influences, he may lose confidence in his large and continuous motions and resort to jerky, isolated little motions (Fig. 13). This frequently happens when children are asked to draw something "real," or if they are shown "how to draw." The child gets some imitative notion. He wants to do the same thing he has seen. Since he is unable to do it, he resorts to a substitute. It may be a substitute for an apple or for writing a letter.

There is another cause for jerky motions. The free and flexible approach toward movement can be seen in the unrestricted free motions in children's scribblings. If the child loses his flexibility and can no longer freely engage in new motions, he withdraws into a rigid repetition of little jerks. In them he does not need to expose himself to new motions. He can continue with one kind of motion which is repeated over and over again. Such little jerks then show inhibitions and lack of adjustment on the part of the child. Suggestions like, "Johnny, let's dance on the paper," or, "Let's run around on the paper," may establish his confidence.

MY CHILD'S SCRIBBLES ARE SMALL
ALTHOUGH HE HAS A LARGE PAPER

Scribblings are as different as children are. Some are determined and bold with large motions; others are dainty and timid in approach.

Let us find out what happens to Johnny when he uses only the corner of his paper or a small area of it (Fig. 14a). There are two possibilities; either Johnny is used to small motions and cannot quickly adjust to a larger sheet of paper, or he sees only the part with which he is concerned, and becomes so absorbed in it that he does not notice the rest of the paper. Certainly, in either case the child does not quickly adjust to the given situation.

However, we have to keep in mind that, while it may be desirable to encourage free and large motions, not all children may be happy with them. Some children feel happier and more secure with a smaller sheet of paper, just as some people feel more secure in a small room. A child may engage in free but small motion, just as another child may engage in free but large motion. We should not regiment a child into drawing big motions. However, it may help the child in his flexibility to give him paper of different sizes. Since the size of the paper influences the child with regard to the size of his motion, different sizes of paper will promote greater flexibility on the part of the child.

If, however, the child uses only a small portion of the paper, regardless of its size, because he "withdraws" into a corner, the child's feeling of security needs to be strengthened! More attention, love, and first of all the freedom of doing things independently may soon alleviate this condition.

14a   My child scribbles small although he has a large paper.   (See page 73)

14b   My child covers the whole paper equally.   (See page 75)   Courtesy Detroit
Public Schools.

MY CHILD COVERS THE WHOLE PAPER EQUALLY

There are two distinct ways in which children usually cover the whole paper equally. We can easily distinguish them if we carefully watch our child. Since each has a different meaning, I should like to discuss them (Fig. 14b).

One child may start his scribbling, and without interrupting continue until the whole sheet of paper is equally covered. The attribute which relates to this rather monotonous activity is a certain perseverance which the child without any doubt possesses.

Another child may start out with one big motion and, as he looks at the paper, become sensitive to the "one-sided" distribution of his motion and thus enlarge his motions toward that part of the paper which he has not yet covered. This child has an unconscious feeling for proper organization. Organization, however, is an important part of a feeling for aesthetics. Without doubt this child is the more creatively inclined child, for he "feels" the motion in relationship to the area on which it is drawn.

MY CHILD SCRIBBLES ON THE WALLS

Scribbling, as we have seen, provides your child with a very important outlet. To prohibit scribbling would not only be detrimental to your child, but may have serious consequences. But there is no reason whatsoever for your child to scribble on your walls if you provide him with proper material and space. Some progressive schools advocate that a certain wall with a washable or specially treated surface should be placed at the disposal of the child. But they forget that the child may not make the same distinctions that we make. Once a child gets used to scribbling on a wall, it is difficult to explain to him that he must not scribble on another wall. The proper material, as will be discussed on page 80, together with some proper space in the house, should be sufficient to give the child enough outlet so that he will not need to scribble on walls. It is senseless and harmful to prohibit such an important activity as scribbling merely for the sake of convenience. If the child has been given the necessary facilities, he must get used to being a part of the group, and should comply with certain orders.

MY CHILD SAYS, "THIS IS A TRAIN," OR, "THIS IS MY DOLL,"
BUT I CAN'T SEE ANYTHING BUT SCRIBBLING

One day Mary may start to tell us a story about her scribbling (Fig. 15). She may say, "This is my doll," and while she makes another motion, she may add, "and she has long hair and is sleeping." This is of the highest significance in Mary's further development, for it is an indication that her thinking obviously has undergone a complete change. Previously, she was not thinking of anything outside herself while she was scribbling. Now her thinking has changed. She thinks of her doll, of something outside her. She now thinks in terms of mental pictures, of images. This change from thinking in terms of motions to thinking in terms of pictures is of decisive significance because from now on, throughout Mary's whole life, most of her thinking will refer to images. In fact, we can scarcely think of a noun, or of a past experience, without referring to a mental picture.

15 My child says, "This is my house." or, "This is my doll," but I can't see anything but scribbling.

That Mary still scribbles while she thinks of her doll only indicates that she is not yet ready to relate her thinking to her drawing. She apparently *is* getting ready for it, and is at the stage in between, where her thinking is somewhat ahead of her actual accomplishment.

It can be easily understood that any discouragement in her thinking would only delay her development and prevent her from gaining the necessary confidence to establish a relationship between her thinking and drawing. We will, therefore, be very happy when Mary starts to talk about her doll while she is scribbling. We shall let her know that we appreciate this important step in her development by listening to her stories. If Mary tells us, "This is my doll, and she has long hair and is sleeping," we shall try to encourage her in her thinking by continuing the trend of thought by asking, "Does your doll sleep in her bed? Does she have a pillow under her head?" Such questions will encourage her to know that her thinking is in the right direction. Of course, we don't expect her to do anything yet but scribble. Yet we shall see that it will not take Mary long before she draws scribbling which is more and more suggestive. She may make round lines for the head and long lines for the legs, and thus establish a relationship to her doll not only in her thinking but in her drawing. Whenever such a relationship is established, the child moves out of the scribbling stage.

HOW LONG SHOULD MY CHILD KEEP ON SCRIBBLING?

Children usually begin to scribble at two years of age. This, like everything in human development, varies from individual to individual. One child may begin to scribble at one and a half years. Because of this, he is by no means a "genius"; in the same way, another, who begins at two and one half, is not retarded. The average age for scribbling lasts from two to four years. Between three and four, children usually give a name to their scribbling, that is, they connect mental pictures with it.

It is without any doubt a sign of advanced development if a child already paints recognizable things at less than three years. It must, however, be kept in mind that this is not always of advantage to the child. If this advancement has been achieved by sacrificing his confidence in his motions, thus depriving the child of a vital experience, it is definitely detrimental to the child's growth. It cannot be stressed enough that we must not push our children in their development. The child must set the pace, and we can only remove the blocks which are in the way of his proper development.

Children should usually have finished scribbling when they are between four and five years of age. Children who still scribble at six, however, often catch up quickly in their development. Children who have had difficulties in their coordination, or who have otherwise been restricted, may stay longer with scribbling. If scribbling, however, is continued beyond six years of age, and no sign of any recognizable objects is present, it is indicative of the child's lack of desire to relate his thinking to images. It is then suggested that the teacher or a school psychologist be consulted.

WHAT HAPPENS IF MY CHILD DOES NOT ENGAGE IN SCRIBBLING AT ALL?

Children usually start their creative experiences with scribbling. In some cases children appear to have "skipped" scribbling and begun with the drawing of recognizable objects. In most cases, it can be found that the child did his scribbling at one point or another in sand or in his cereal and that the parents did not recognize it as such. If scribbling apparently has been omitted in the child's development, it is suggested that the child be given an opportunity to engage in activities which permit him to assure himself of control of his motions. Finger painting is an excellent means of "introducing" motions at a time when the child apparently has grown out of it. In the section on materials, we shall talk about the use of finger painting. While this introduction of motions, in cases where the child apparently has skipped them, may not be necessary, it is a good precautionary measure.

SHALL I GIVE MY CHILD CLAY OR OTHER MATERIALS?

The child should at all times have experiences with as many different materials as possible. Different materials of different textures and consistency enrich the child's sensitivity in using his sense of touch.

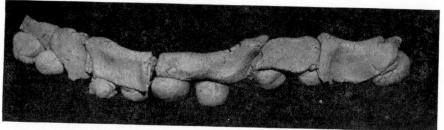

16a My child calls his piece of clay a "train." (See page 80) Courtesy of Educational Project, Museum of Modern Art, New York.

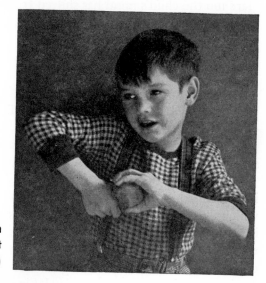

16b In modeling, the child can do many things which he cannot do in painting. (See page 80)

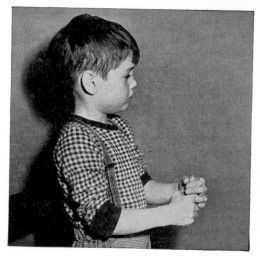

16c Without looking at his work he touches and feels the form.

Even if he merely pounds or kneads lumps of clay, it promotes the child's ability to coordinate his motions. There comes a time, however, when he wants to assure himself that he can control his forming of equal balls, coils, or "pies." During this period we can see children form countless rows of such "pies." They serve the important purpose of developing self-confidence in the child's ability to be master of his manipulative ability, to control his forming hands. Again, as in scribbling, one day the child may pick up a lump of clay, and while "zooming" it through the air, say, "This is an airplane." This is the stage corresponding to the stage in which the child tells stories while he scribbles. Here too the child's mind has shifted from the mere activity of forming to thinking in terms of images (Figs. 16a, 16b, and 16c).

WHAT ART MATERIALS SHOULD I GIVE TO MY SCRIBBLING CHILD?

Remember that we said that only those art materials which help him satisfy his needs are good for your child.

As we have seen, one of the main needs of your child in his scribbling is to satisfy his desire for movement and the control of it. A material which does not help your child in this is not a good one. For instance, if we were to give him water color, he would end up with motions which, because of the "running" and merging quality of fluid water color, would render an undistinguishable blurred mass of color in which no single motion can be recognized. Since your child cannot distinguish them, he cannot satisfy his desire for control and coordination (Fig. 17).

Crayon serves the need for control excellently. As the child moves his crayon on the paper, he can control, guide, and direct his motion. He does not even need many colors. They would only make him stop his activity for the mere sake of changing them. Thick crayons are preferable to thin ones. Remember that we said to break the thin ones to avoid careful, timid handling.

To avoid monotony, and also to give children a variety of experiences, besides his desire for control of motions, give him poster paint or show-card paint (not too thin, to prevent running). He will enjoy the feeling of the material. Although it will not promote his desire for motor control, it will give him emotional satisfaction and enjoyment, for he will love the possibilities of paint. His imagination will be greatly stimulated by this medium, especially when he starts to tell you stories about his scribbling, but he may also use it as an emotional outlet. For instance, if he has aggressive feelings toward his younger brother he may paint over the symbol which stands for his brother, as it were, to get rid of him. Such substitute action may relieve the child of his aggressive feelings.

17 My child ends up with a blurred mass of color. (See page 80)

A popular medium, especially in kindergarten, is finger paint. Finger paint is commercially available, but you also can prepare it yourself quite easily by mixing paint powder or poster paint with starch boiled with water. Add some soap flakes. Have smooth, well glued paper. (Finger-paint paper is commercially available also.) White wrapping paper with a smooth waxy surface is good. Spread your starch smoothly and thinly on it, mix some paint into it, and by making motions with your hands and fingers you achieve stimulating results. Some thought, however, should be given to the following discussion. As you know, there are certain stages in early infancy during which the child likes to play with dirt or even with his own excrement. There is nothing wrong about this, and if the child needs it as outlet we may even provide him with a pail of wet sand. If your child, however, has grown out of this stage and, like every child, develops a desire to use tools, then finger paint, because of its very consistency, may remind your child of these former stages, and retard his development. You may easily see this effect by watching your child. If he is more concerned with the sticky con-sistency and with smearing the paint all over than with using it to enjoy his motions, he definitely is not using finger paint to satisfy his desire for controlling his movements.

If your child, however, is tense, timid, and fearful, finger painting may give him an important outlet even when used in the above-described manner.

the 4-7 year old

As YOUR child grows, he no longer is satisfied with a mere fictitious relationship between his thinking in pictures and his drawing or painting. He actually would like to establish a "real" relationship. "Look, my daddy has a head and two big legs"; therefore, "My drawing *is* Daddy." He has established for the first time a *"real"* relationship. For the child, at least, it is as "real" as our adult relationships are. Everyone knows that Johnny knows more of his daddy than that he has a head and two big legs, but during the process of drawing this was to him emotionally most outstanding. That Daddy has big legs apparently is his most important characteristic in Johnny's mind as the child draws.

As Johnny grows, his relationships to his environment change. The more sensitive and alert he becomes, the more things will be important to him. Daddy may have guided him across the street, and while holding and feeling his bare hands Johnny may become conscious of them as an important experience belonging to Daddy. When Johnny draws again, he thinks differently. "Daddy has a head and two big legs; he also has two big hands (to guide me across the street)." As Johnny's relation-

18   My child discovers that he can draw "real things."   (See page 83)

ships become more intricate, his paintings and drawings become more differentiated (Fig. 19).

Since Johnny has only just discovered that he can establish a "real" relationship between objects and his paintings, it would certainly be too much for him to establish an order in his drawing at the same time. He draws or paints his objects in the sequence in which they come to his mind. After a visit to the zoo, he may want to paint the zoo. He does not paint a particular impression; he merely enumerates whatever he can think of while he is painting. "I was in the zoo. There am I; there is a giraffe; there is an elephant; there is a cage." Obviously the different animals or objects are in no particular relationship in the painting. They appear dispersed. Yet, for the child, another relationship has been very definitely established: the relationship between the zoo and his drawing. It does not even occur to the child that he is standing in front of the cage of the giraffe and that the giraffe was quite a distance from the elephant. These *spatial* relationships don't bother him. He is too busy discovering that a giraffe has a long neck and spots, and that his animal has a long neck and spots; therefore his animal *is* a giraffe.

If we were to disturb the child in this important discovery that he

19 "As Johnny grows, the relationship to his environment changes." (See page 84) Courtesy Detroit Public Schools.

can establish a relationship between his own drawing and the outside by calling his attention to a spatial relationship, he would only become confused and lose confidence in his own discovery. "But Johnny, you were standing in *front* of the giraffe's cage," is the type of criticism which disturbs Johnny.

If Johnny, however, has developed a close emotional tie to an object, such as his cat (Fig. 20), he *will* put himself in relationship to it. On the basis of emotional ties, the child easily establishes spatial relationships in his paintings, and we shall see that the things he paints are no longer meaninglessly dispersed on the paper.

20 A good motivation makes the child more sensitive to his environment. (See page 85) Courtesy Grand Rapids, Michigan, Public Schools.

WHEN SHOULD MY CHILD START TO DRAW FIGURES AND OBJECTS?

As has been said previously, the drawing of recognizable objects and figures depends upon the child's desire to establish a relationship between his drawing and the outside world. If the child is not ready for this step into the outside world, he should by no means be forced to do so. Just as you would not like to be forced to step into the unknown, the child also becomes frustrated if he is told to relate himself to the outside world while he still is concerned with his own little self, his own movements and how to control them. The *child* has to determine the time when he wants to relate himself to outside experiences in his paintings. *We* can only help him to establish more and more sensitive relationships. *It is not important* if one child establishes these relationships one year sooner and another one year later. It is much more important for the child that he is not frustrated in his own discoveries and experiences. Ten years from now, it will be very important for him whether he has been frustrated in his independent thinking, in his establishment of proper coordination of movements. It cannot be emphasized enough that pushing your child is the most harmful custom in today's education. Don't be impatient! Your child will be an adult soon enough. But it is altogether different whether your child becomes one of the five millions who at one time or another are mentally or emotionally ill, or whether he will become an independently thinking and creative physicist, an engineer, a physician, a businessman, a housewife or a worker.

Between four or five years of age, the average child starts to relate his thinking to the outside world and to draw figures and objects. As has been said before, if your child starts at three or earlier, it is no indication that he is a "genius." On the contrary, it may well be that he has not had enough scribbling. If your child still scribbles at six, it does not mean that he is retarded. It may merely mean that he *needed* the time to establish the necessary confidence. If your child, however, still scribbles at seven, it is advisable that you consult the teacher or the school psychologist. At seven years of age all children should relate their thinking to imagery.

HOW CAN I HELP MY CHILD IN "IMPROVING" HIS PAINTINGS?

We must first make sure that we both understand the same thing by "improving." Improving does not mean more pleasing to my adult taste. It does not deal, as we shall see, with the final product at all. The "improvement" of my child's creative art work depends on two important factors during this period of development. The one deals with the establishment of more differentiated relationships, the other with the child's ability to relate things to each other spatially. More differentiated relationships can only be obtained through greater sensitivity toward these objects.

Our motivations then must consist of making the child more sensitive through experiences which reach him. For instance, if you recognize that Johnny never draws the nose in his figures, consciousness of the nose would certainly make him add one. "Johnny, remember when it was so cold outside that when you went to school all your fingers were stiff? Where else did you feel it? In your nose? How did it feel? Let's paint the time it was so cold that our noses froze." No child would omit the nose after such motivation! But do not say, "Johnny, you did not draw the nose." That would not establish a more sensitive relationship, nor would it give him an opportunity to discover it for himself. Only through individual experiences will the child grow in his sensitive relationships. At another time you may notice that the tree which Johnny is drawing has only a trunk and two big branches, but no twigs. Let us think of a meaningful experience which Johnny had with a twig. "Johnny, remember when you were jumping beneath a tree and you wanted to pull yourself up on a branch. What happened? Oh, it broke? What broke? Why? It was too thin. Let's draw when you tried to hold on to the tree and you fell off."

After such motivations Johnny may or may not include the part to which he has been made more sensitive. If he does not include it, this is a sign that he is not ready for it and that the motivation did not reach him. It is also very common for the child to include the part to which he has been "sensitized" but to omit it again shortly after the motivation. This means that the child's relationship to this part has not become of permanent significance. It is like learning the meaning of a new word! As long as the word is not a part of your vocabulary, you cannot use it. However, if you hear the word in different connections it will gradually become *your* word. The same is true with Johnny. If he becomes "sensitized" to the same part in different ways, it finally *will* become his own property. If such motivations are a frequent occurrence, your child will not only become more sensitive and alert toward his environment, but he will become more flexible in his expression as his "vocabulary of forms" grows. The more "forms" he has at his disposal, the more easily will he express himself. It is this flexibility of expression which has a decisive influence on his emotional growth and his total personality.

MY CHILD DOES NOT RELATE THINGS TO EACH OTHER; HE JUST DISPERSES THEM

As has been said before, the child establishes his first relationships between objects through his emotional participation, interest, and drive. If Mary likes her doll, it will be quite self-evident that she draws herself holding her doll. If John likes his bike, he will most easily establish his relationship to the bike in his painting.

21a My child does not relate things to each other. (See page 90)

21b My child only relates things to each other when they are emotionally significant to him. Courtesy Duke of York School, Toronto, Canada.

If we see that our child has difficulty in establishing proper relationships between objects in his painting, the best motivation is one in
which the emotional relationship to an object is emphasized. "Mary,
show me in your painting how you love your doll. Do you hug her?
How do you hug her? Show it to me in your painting." If such an immediate relationship has been established, a motivation which includes
objects which are not as intimately related will reach her more easily.
"Mary, be careful that you don't wake up your doll when you push
her carriage; just push it gently. Show me how you push it gently in
your painting" (Figs. 21a, 21b).

It is needless to say that in most cases the child will provide himself
with the necessary experience and motivation which will lead him to
the recognition of "spatial relationships" without any additional stimulus
on your part, provided that the child has not been restricted or inhibited by outside influences. But since most of our children have been
exposed to detrimental influences in schools, homes, or through coloring
books, some additional motivations on your part will certainly help your
child in his self-confidence.

21c   Johnny learns through his own experiences.

From the foregoing paragraphs it becomes evident that the improvement of the child's creative work occurs only through the child's development of his personality, and not as an independent factor. To show the child technical "tricks," or to help him by actively painting or drawing into his work, would only mean interfering with the child's own ability to discover and think for himself. It would also take away his own initiative and self-confidence necessary to solve his problems. All these are attributes which are highly important for his development, his future happiness and success. We all know how individuals suffer when they have never learned to apply their own thinking and imagination to what they do.

MY CHILD PAINTS A SKY YELLOW, A FIGURE BLUE, ETC.

Just as Johnny may not relate objects to each other when he is concentrating on establishing a relationship between the object and his drawings, so may he fail when he relates the color to the object while he paints (Fig. 22). This is quite natural, and no parent should interfere with the child's own discovery of color-object relationships by telling the child the "right" color. He should never say: "Johnny, a sky is not yellow. Can't you see that?" Johnny is too involved in establishing a relationship between "Daddy" and his drawings. The sky was insignificant. He painted it yellow only because there is a sky and he enjoys yellow.

Gradually, however, Johnny will discover color relationships. He will discover them for himself, first with things which are important to him. Johnny has received a red toy car as a birthday present. He likes it very much. When he paints it in one of his paintings, he paints it red because it is *his* car and his car *is* red. This is important to Johnny because the car would not be his car if it were not red. Again we see that children establish their first color relationships to objects on the basis of the emotional significance which the respective objects have to them. This is important to us because we shall use this point to stimulate color-object relationships. Parents have asked me again and again, "What's wrong with telling our children that a sky is not yellow but blue and that an apple is red?" By doing so you have prevented the child from making the discovery himself: "Look, my apple is as red as the apple is on the tree!" Whenever we can give the child an opportunity to use his mind and imagination independently, we should do so. It is wrong to take this important initiative from the child and "feed him his knowledge with a spoon." Furthermore, it is not important at all whether the child arrives at an understanding of the relationships of colors and objects one month sooner or later. Always consider what will be of significance for your child ten years from now. In ten years no one will ask whether your child established the relationships of objects and colors when he was five, six, or seven years old. It will, however, be an important part of his personality whether he uses his mind independently or whether he has become conditioned to the fact that every decision and discovery is made for him.

If we desire to promote the relationships of colors and objects, we must think of motivations in which color is emotionally significant to the child. "Mary, remember that when we were in the orchard I told you not to pick the green apples. They are not ripe; they are sour; let's pick only the red ones. Let's paint how you pick the red apples only." If the child still does not paint the apples red, it is an indication that the motivation either has not reached the child or that the child is not yet ready for perceiving colors in relation to objects. If he were ready but simply did not know the color red (which is rarely the case with a four- to seven-year-old child), he would have asked you, "Is this red?" If such a question comes from the *child*, it is quite logical to give the correct answer. This discovery is, as we have seen, a part of his general growth and development.

MY CHILD DRAWS "OUT OF PROPORTION"

What is in "correct" proportion for the eye may be completely "out of proportion" to our emotions (Fig. 23). Think of a tiny little gnat getting into your eye. How big they both feel, the gnat as well as the eye; and if the eye keeps on hurting, how negligible your foot. You have even forgotten that your foot is a part of your body. In your mind it is completely out of proportion to your hurting eye. Or think of a fever blister which appears just as you are about to go to a party. The other guests scarcely recognize it. For them it is so tiny in proportion to the rest of you that they are unaware of it. For you, however, it can be most annoying, and its subjective feeling may be completely out of proportion to its actual size.

23 "I have a headache." My child draws out of proportion. (See page 92)

For the child, such subjective feelings for proportions are the dominating ones. The proportions which he sees are subordinated to the proportions he feels. In fact, experiments have shown that if a child becomes too self-conscious or inhibited, his visual proportions "improve." This shows that for this period of development it is more natural for the child to draw his proportions according to his feeling and not according to actual measurements. It is quite logical, when a child reaches for something which he wants badly, for his arm to become more important to him than at a time when he kicks a ball with his foot. Consequently, he will draw the reaching arm much larger. He draws it *in proportion* to his feeling for it and *out of proportion* only for an audience which looks at his painting objectively.

HOW CAN I KNOW THE MEANING OF MY CHILD'S ART WORK?

If we speak here of meaning, then we shall confine ourselves to the literal meaning of the art work only. Often, when we look at our child's art work, it appears almost meaningless to us, while he may be very excited about it. He may also happen to work with great concentration on something which we can scarcely recognize. We usually are embarrassed and do not know what to say if Johnny proudly shows us his final product. Feeling obliged to make some statement, we usually say, "You did a wonderful job, Johnny!" Or, what is worse, we say, "Is this an Indian, Johnny?" And Johnny's feelings may be hurt because we did not recognize that he painted himself. Johnny paints himself differently from the way we see him, but he is so involved in his own work that he thinks that *we* see his painting as *he* sees it. But then comes the great disappointment when we see an "Indian" while he sees himself in his painting.

How can we avoid such disappointments, since they obviously do not encourage the child in his work? At the same time, how can we find out the meaning of our child's work?

It becomes apparent that we should never approach our child with suggestive questions, such as, "Is this an Indian?" We should not engage in guesswork. Let the child tell you what he intended to express. "Johnny, tell me something about your painting." But don't be satisfied if Johnny gives you an evasive answer like, "Oh, just something," or when he says, "Oh, I don't know." That he learns to express himself verbally is just as important as his painting. So you have to become more inquisitive by asking more definite questions, such as, "What does this mean?" or, "What is this for?" Of course, you must point to definite parts if you ask such definite questions. Only when you are sure that you know the meaning of the painting, and only when you can identify certain things, should you refer to them. "Yes, Johnny, that's the inn where we stopped on our way home. I, too, remember the telescope through which we looked." Such common participation in experiences is not only encouraging to his work, but also of importance for the establishment of greater confidence in you and your interest in your child.

MUST I BE ABLE TO RECOGNIZE WHAT MY CHILD DRAWS OR PAINTS?

From the previous discussion it becomes clear that the child's world and his representation of it are quite different from our adult world. The world of our children looks strange to us because we have forgotten how it feels to be a child. That we do not recognize our child's work is, therefore, not only understandable, but logical. However, if we remain ignorant of him and his work, we not only miss a great deal of his life, but we may be guilty of not having helped him when he needed help most.

MY CHILD IS AFRAID TO PUT PRESSURE ON HIS CRAYON, OR TO USE PAINT FREELY

Nothing can be more inhibiting to a child than a constant consciousness of his art materials. How often have I seen a proud mother presenting a set of crayons to her child by saying, "Mary, I brought you a new set of crayons, but I wonder how long you can keep them as nice." I have also heard parents and teachers fussing about broken crayons, or even scolding their children. "Yesterday I brought you the set, and today look at it! Two crayons are already broken! You'll wait a long time before you get anything new again!" These are quotations

24   My child is afraid to put pressure on his crayon.   (See page 95)

from actual conversations. No wonder that when the child becomes "crayon conscious" he no longer dares to put pressure on them (Fig. 24). Is not the child's freedom and happiness worth more than money can buy? The freer the child, the less inhibited is he in experimenting with his art materials. Why shouldn't he find out for himself how he can use his crayons with bold lines, with fine lines, with dark shading, with light shading, with the point or with the broad side? Such experimental attitude only encourages his inventiveness, and makes him more flexible and adjustable. These are all attributes which you cannot buy. However, if he becomes intimidated in the free use of his materials he will be afraid to use them at all.

The same holds true for paint. "Mary, you use too much paint! Don't use the whole sheet of paper," are warnings which one can hear again and again. If Mary needs a full brush, she should find out how it looks on the paper. She can only find out by discovering how it differs from a dry brush.

Does this mean that we should let the child waste his material? By no means. But there is a difference between wasting material and using it as efficiently as one can. Wasting also means not learning by not using. For instance, it is a big waste if the child keeps his crayons new by not using them. He wastes his most precious inventiveness, and with it, his freedom. The same is true if he does not use his paint for gaining new experiences.

Before we think of "waste," let us always ask, "Did the child gain by his experience?" If he did not, the material is wasted whether it remains new or whether it is willfully thrown into the gutter!

Whenever the child is afraid to put pressure on his crayons, or to use his paint freely, we can be sure that at some time or another he has been intimidated by wrong criticism.

As has been said before, the best means to counteract such intimidations is to break the crayons before you give them to your child. If necessary, you can play a game with him. "Let's find out what a crayon can do! It can go softly; it can go skating over the whole paper; it can go on its flat side," and so on. This, however, is only suggested if the child has been intimidated and needs an additional stimulus to attain freedom.

It is needless to say that timidity may have different causes. To give the child love and a feeling of security will always be most essential for establishing more confidence in the child's free use of materials.

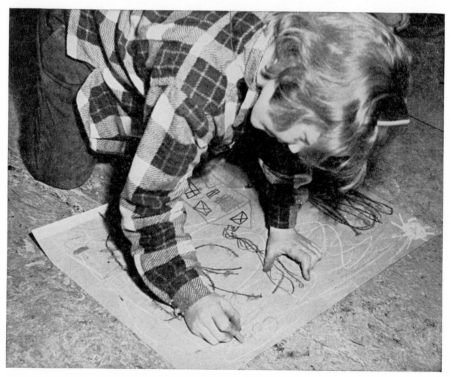

25 My child is completely absorbed in her painting.

26 My child loves to model in clay.

MY CHILD MODELS BY PUTTING SINGLE PIECES OF CLAY TOGETHER

It may never have occurred to you to watch how your child models in clay. Yet if you watch him carefully you will find that he has a very distinct way of modeling. When Johnny makes a "man," he always makes the single parts first, the head, the body, two coils for arms, two for legs, and then he "assembles" them by putting these single parts together. He may even add the features as separate parts. This is the common way that children model. It clearly shows the child's thinking. Johnny says to himself, "A man has a head, a body, two arms, and two legs." As he thinks, so he models. Some children, especially in the very early stages, are satisfied to enumerate the single parts. Consequently, they don't even bother to assemble them. Only when they start to think in terms of relationships, such as, "The arms come from the shoulder; the head is on the shoulder; the legs grow from the body," will they assemble the single pieces. So that the pieces hold together well, tell your child to wet the ends and press them firmly together without harming the form.

As we shall see later, it is very important that you do not influence your child to change his "technique." Thinking in "single parts" is different from thinking of the "whole," and a superficially enforced change of "technique" may confuse the child's thinking (Fig. 27).

MY CHILD MODELS BY STARTING WITH THE WHOLE LUMP OF CLAY

Starting with the whole lump of clay and pulling out the single details, such as legs, arms, and other parts, are found more rarely among children. But there are children who quite naturally think first of the whole figure and then of its details. Most adults think this way. If we imagine a tree, we most commonly first think of the whole tree, and then of its details, its trunk, its branches, its twigs, and the kind of foliage it has. In fact, if we look at something we first have a total impression of the "whole" and then we see the details. Observation consists of getting first the total impression and then the details. We see first the whole tree, then the branches, the twigs, and the leaves. Indeed, we can find the observers among those children who first model the whole and then the details.

It is needless to say that changing the technique of these children would confuse their thinking just as changing the technique of children who assemble their modeling from single details confuses them (Fig. 28).

SHOULD MY CHILD DO ART WORK OTHER THAN PAINTING?

Whether the child builds in sand, whether he pastes things together, or whether he tinkers whenever he applies his mind creatively, he engages in an art activity. There are countless other possibilities besides painting, drawing, and modeling which will serve the child's creative needs. Certainly, he can also show his independent thinking, flexibility, inventiveness, and imagination when he invents a "construction" out

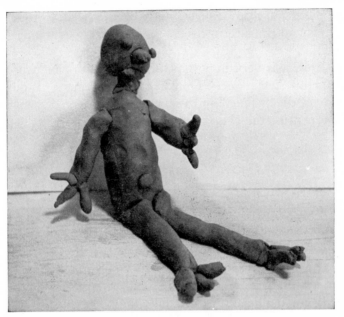

27 My child starts his modeling with single details. (See page 99)

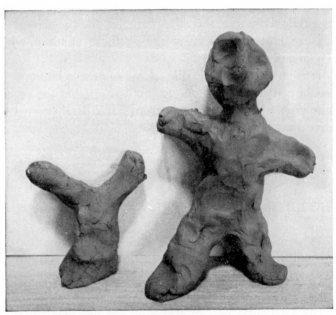

28 My child starts his modeling with the whole lump of clay. (See page 99)

of cardboard, toothpicks, buttons, and all kinds of other materials (Fig. 29). Give your child enough scrap material and he will start using it as an important part of his imaginative activity. However, since painting, drawings, and clay modeling more directly serve the child's need for confronting him with his own emotional experiences, this book deals mainly with these three types of expression.

29 Children love to do construction work. (See page 99) Courtesy of Children's Art Classes, Art Museum of Montreal, Canada.

MUST I SAVE MY CHILD'S PAINTINGS AND MODELINGS?

As he matures, the child's art expression changes. Actually, the most important part for his growth occurs during the process while he creates. In many instances the child loses his attachment to his work almost as soon as he is finished with it. There is no need for the adult to prolong artificially the period of close attachment. I have seen countless children who could not even identify their paintings after two or three months. There is definitely no need to save the creative works for the child's sake. In fact, to confront the child with his former work again and again may have the detrimental effect of paying too much attention to the final product. Especially with regard to modelings, where the saving may become a storage problem, it is of no advantage *to the child* to save his work beyond the period of his *immediate attachment*. It is needless to say that no creative work should be destroyed in the presence of the child. It is always good to save the last few works in order to avoid any ill feelings.

It is, however, of great advantage and interest *to you* to save the creative work of your children, especially drawings and paintings, which can easily be put into a folder. They not only show you the creative development of your child, but they will also help you in guiding him. For this purpose it is advisable that you write on the back of the painting the date of the work, a brief description of what it represents, and whatever comments the child makes. It is suggested that you do not do this in the presence of your child. It would only make him too self-conscious, and may create a feeling of being controlled. If you look at the work of your child in the sequence in which it was done, you can often detect periods in which the child apparently retrogresses. By comparing the paintings with former works, you may see less interest, less identification with the subject. You may immediately have the feeling that the paintings look "empty" as compared with the former ones. This may give you an important clue that something apparently upsetting is going on in the child. Conversely, you may also discover a sudden gain of interest, when the paintings look "richer."

There is another important reason why you should save your children's art work, a reason which is often neglected today because it is of no immediate significance. One never knows what may occur in the future, but if childhood records of an objective nature, like children's drawings, can be produced, they may prove important in instances of later emotional disturbances.

Needless to say, there is also a sentimental value if you attach to your children's work some snapshots which correspond to the age levels of the work.

WHAT MATERIALS SHOULD I BUY?

As has been said before, the best material is the one which most helps the child in his expression. Inasmuch as the child's desire is to establish some kind of relationship between his work and the object, the material should help him in this desire. Often such relationships do not consist of "outlines" only, but require the covering of larger areas. Larger areas cannot be as easily covered with crayon as with paint. Therefore a bristle brush (¼″ wide), poster, or show-card paint in a limited selection (yellow, red, blue, green, brown, black, white) and absorbent paper (newsprint) would be the best material. A set of crayons, as indicated previously, will always be helpful for art work, which can be done when a limited time only is at the child's disposal.

The plastic bag with clay should always be filled.

Finger paintings can now be used with no distracting influences. The child is too remote from his early childhood stages to be reminded of dirt-like consistencies. (See page 81.)

Of course, the scrap box is always a source for creative ideas. The richer it is with materials of different textures, shapes, and consistency, the better will it lend itself to creative ideas.

the 7-10 year old

As JOHNNY grows, he improves the relationships between his drawings and the things which he represents. He has become more aware of his environment through the many experiences to which he has been exposed.

There comes a time, however, when Johnny no longer feels like establishing increasingly complex relationships. He arrives at a period wherein it becomes natural for him to need the self-assurance that he can draw a tree, a house, or other things more than he needs the continuous change of his concepts. We can easily see this need when Johnny or Mary always draws the same kind of trees or figures. They change them only when they have something definite to express.

Johnny will arrive at the period in which he is satisfied with his tree or his figure at a different time than Mary does. Of course, they will have arrived at different concepts for trees, houses, or figures. Mary was more alert than Johnny. Therefore Mary's trees, houses, or figures are more differentiated than Johnny's (Figs. 30 and 31). Virginia may have arrived much earlier at the stage in which she no longer feels the

30 "Johnny's figures and flowers are less differentiated than Mary's." (See page 104)

31 "Mary's figures and flowers are more differentiated than Johnny's." (See page 104)   Courtesy Public Schools, Pittsburgh, Pa.

desire "for changes" because Virginia never liked to expose herself to new experiences. Her trees, houses, and figures are very poor. The trees have no branches, the houses no windows, and her figures no hands or feet—just sticks attached to an oval "body." Apparently Virginia needed the "self-assurance" that she *can* draw a tree, a man, or a house at too early a time, when her sensitivity toward the things which she wants to paint had not been developed.

This shows that the longer we can keep our children flexible toward their experiences, the more differentiated will their paintings be when they arrive at the stage where they feel the need to assure themselves of their concepts. Thus, arriving at this stage at an early period is by no means an advantage. On the contrary, it will only be found in children who need such self-assurance for lack of emotional security.

However we may try to motivate our children for a more flexible and sensitive creative expression, sooner or later—but somewhere between seven and nine years of age—the child will need this period of rest in which he repeats the same type of figure. Every achievement becomes an achievement only when it grows out of the accidental realm into the realm of consciousness. We do not believe in our achievements unless, *through repetition*, we convince ourselves of our mastery. Our children, too, assure themselves through repetition that they have arrived at a definite representation of a man, a tree, a house, and so on. But only when Johnny does not intend to express something definite will he draw his trees or men alike; that is, when he thinks, That is a tree, or That is a man. However, when he thinks, This man is big and this one is small, Johnny will change his drawing concept for man. Johnny may draw a "big man" by giving him long legs; Mary, however, may draw a "big man" by enlarging everything, body, arms, legs, and the head uniformly; while Virginia may only enlarge the head. The differences with which these children express "larger" or "smaller" are indicative of their personalities. A study of the kinds of change with which the child expresses his experiences would allow us to understand the intention underlying the child's creative work. In another book I have attempted to give a careful account of these changes and their meaning for personality growth.* It would be beyond the purpose of this book to include them in this discussion. It is, however, of great importance to us to notice that these changes have a great significance to the child and should by no means be "corrected."

* *Creative and Mental Growth*, rev. ed.. New York. The Macmillan Company, 1952.

MY CHILD STILL DRAWS OUT OF PROPORTION

From the previous chapter it becomes quite logical that the child has almost no other means at his disposal for showing the importance of a particular part except to exaggerate it in size (Fig. 32). If Mary loves her doll, the size in which she draws her doll will adequately express this. If Mary is afraid of dropping the doll, she will draw herself holding it tightly. How else could she change her concept of herself except by exaggerating her hands? Thus, exaggeration of important parts is a natural means of expression at this period of development. In fact, as has been pointed out previously, if the child *always* draws "correct" proportions it would appear that the child is emotionally untouched by her experiences.

The natural response to an experience which affects the child emotionally is that the child "changes" his concept of the part with which he is emotionally concerned. One of these "changes" is that he exaggerates this part. This is particularly true for two types of experiences: one, when the child considers the object very important, as in the case of Mary's doll; the other, when the child considers body feelings important. Such exaggerations of single parts of the body usually give adults the feeling of being "out of proportion," but actually this is merely a shift of emphasis from visual proportioning to emotionally determined size relationships. If you have a headache you, too, feel that your head is larger. That you don't draw it larger is only due to inhibitions, and too much self-control. Yet if your head feels larger, it may be the "truest" form of expression to draw it according to your feeling. The child has no inhibitions or self-awareness. Therefore his considerations with regard to the final product do not exist. The most natural form of expression for him, then, is to draw a head larger which feels larger. To correct such a form of expression would only mean changing a true and sincere feeling to an imposed rigid form of measuring which obviously is meaningless to the child.

What has been said about "exaggeration" is also true for the "neglect" or "omission" of parts. Usually a definite emotional reaction is responsible for such changes. It is needless to say that correcting them would only deprive the child of his experiences.

32 **"Putting on the Light." My child still draws out of proportion.** (See page 107) Courtesy Public Schools, Toronto, Canada.

MY CHILD DRAWS EVERYTHING ON A LINE,
OR ON THE EDGE OF THE PAPER

In many of your child's drawings you may see that all objects, such as houses, trees, figures, and cars are standing on a line or on the edge of the paper. You may wonder why your child is doing this, since such a line actually does not exist in nature (Fig. 33).

As your child grows, his awareness of his environment grows also; he also realizes increasingly that it possesses order. When he was younger he enumerated and recognized only environmental objects: "There is a tree, a house, a car." In his paintings the objects were either meaninglessly dispersed, or brought into some emotional relationship to the child. Johnny, when he is between seven and ten years old, no longer thinks merely in terms of enumerating objects; he also brings a certain objective order into them. He realizes that objects have some spatial relationship to one another. He now thinks: I am on the street; the tree is on the street; *we all are on the street.* Since the line, or the edge of

33   My child draws everything on a line.

the paper, represents the base on which all things stand, in this case the street, he places all objects on it.

The first realization that he is part of a larger environment is a very important experience. It indicates that he has become conscious of the fact that he is no longer concerned merely with his own self; he has also discovered that he is part of a larger whole, and relates himself to an "orderly" environment. The importance of this new feeling for orderly relationships can be realized only when its implications for our child are understood.

As long as we do not realize the meaning of our environment, and as long as we do not relate ourselves to it, we are not ready for active cooperation. Indeed, recent studies have brought out that children who do not relate themselves to their environment in their art are usually the children who have difficulty in cooperating with their environment.

There is still another implication that is especially important for parents. The ability of your child to relate things in his art is the same ability which he uses, in reading, in relating letters or words. If you can make your child more sensitive in his ability to relate things in his drawings or paintings, he may improve his reading. Needless to say, making the child more sensitive does not mean "showing" him relationships, thus, "Can't you see that you and Mary are standing on the lawn and that the tree grows out of it?" The child must *discover* such relationships through his own experiences. Only then will they be meaningful to him.

Drawing objects or persons on one base line or on the edge of the paper appears, then, to be a natural and healthy sign.

MY CHILD'S ART LOOKS STIFF

A form of expression in which there is a tendency to repeat the same concepts with little variation may easily be considered "stiff." Yet it is very important to distinguish whether "stiffness" is part of this natural tendency, or whether it is due to the inability of the child to use his concepts flexibly and to change them according to individual experiences. Johnny's drawings may appear "stiff" because whenever he draws a man he draws him in the same way, although he changes parts wherever an experience determines such a change. This mode of expression (Figs. 34 and 35) is quite natural for this level, and therefore we

34 My child's drawing looks stiff to me.

Children Swimming   Jane- 7yrs

35 My child does not put motion into his figures.

should not consider it "stiff." However, Virginia may repeat the same forms again and again without permitting an experience to change one of her concepts. Therefore all her figures are pure repetitions. Such "stiffness" is not natural, but indicative of some kind of emotional maladjustment.

Another factor that contributes to an apparent stiffness is the base line. When all objects are standing on a line, the picture will appear stiffer than if they were distributed over the whole paper. However, this "stiffness" is also a natural part of the development of the child.

MY CHILD STILL DOES NOT RELATE THE THINGS
IN HIS DRAWINGS TO ONE ANOTHER

Before we say that our child does not relate the objects in his drawing to one another, let us find out whether this is based on facts. How can I see that my child does not relate things?

36   My child draws objects meaninglessly dispersed.

If the objects are meaninglessly dispersed on the paper (Fig. 36) it is quite clear that no attempt has been made to relate them to one another. If a child between seven and ten years of age does not show a desire to relate things, it is a sign that he does not feel the need to see or recognize their relationships. Since the child under normal conditions develops this desire, something must have interfered. If this occurs in the later period, that is, between eight and ten, it is recommended that the school psychologist be consulted.

If the child does not use base lines for his "spatial order," it does not mean that he has not established it by other means. Any relationship between objects which the child establishes should be recognized as such. If the child places a chair next to the table, this spatial relationship is as meaningful as that of the base line. An experience similar to that which makes him relate the chair to the table is also responsible for his desire to relate many objects to their base. The difference between both experiences lies mainly in the fact that the one is a single relationship, while the relationship to a common base indicates a group relationship. Since it is important for the child to discover any form of relationship, for in his life the ability to relate things will play an important role, the motivation of experiences which contain relationships is very important. "Remember, Johnny, that when we were in the zoo we passed the cages? Which animal was in the first? Which next? Which after that? Let's paint how we pass the cages." Such suggestions immediately lead to a better understanding and to a greater awareness of relationships. This, in turn, motivates the child to establish better spatial relationships in his painting.

MY CHILD ALWAYS PAINTS THE SKY AT THE TOP OF THE PAPER

As long as the child is not visually aware of his environment, that is, as long as he evaluates his environment in terms of what it *means* to him he will not paint what he sees, but what things mean to him. Johnny may think: I am standing on the ground, the sky is above, and the air is in between. Consequently the child will paint the ground at the bottom of the paper, the sky at the top, and what is in between he will leave "empty" (Fig. 37). This is actually a much more logical concept than the one where the sky meets the earth at the horizon. Since this is a natural form of expression, a "correction" would only mean an interference with the child's independent thinking.

37 My child always paints the sky on the top of the paper. (See page 113)

As soon as the child becomes visually aware of his environment, he will discover for himself that the sky apparently meets the earth at the horizon.

MY CHILD ALWAYS PAINTS THE SKY WITH A SUN

It is quite common, especially in early childhood, for children never to separate the sun from the sky in their paintings. For many children, the sun belongs to the sky just as much as the eyes to the head of a man which they paint. The sun has become a part of the concept of the sky. How much the two belong together can be seen in paintings in which, in spite of an apparent storm or rain, the sun still remains a part of the blue sky. The black clouds are merely drawn over it.

As soon as the child begins to use his powers of observation, he will no longer think in terms of concepts. He will then observe that the sun is not always a part of the sky. As a result he will paint the sky differently. It would only deprive the child of his own discovery if we were to tell him not to draw the sun at all times. At a period in which it is of significance that the child assure himself of his individually established concepts, it will only affect his self-confidence if we interfere with his discoveries.

MY CHILD SOMETIMES DRAWS THINGS UPSIDE DOWN OR AT AN ANGLE

It appears odd to see children turn their paper around in order to draw or paint carefully the other side of the street "upside down" (Fig. 38). While this procedure may seem rather strange to us, it constitutes

38 "Policeman Guiding the Traffic." Look at the people "on both sides of the street." The child turned around to paint the "other side." Courtesy Duke of York School, Toronto, Canada.

a most interesting expression of a feeling for space. Mary, standing in the middle of the street, has often thought: I have houses to my right and I have also houses to my left. When she comes home to draw them, she draws first the two sides of the street. Of course, she uses two base lines. Then she draws the house "to her left." In order to draw the houses better in this position, she turns the paper so that they appear upright (Fig. 38). To paint the houses at her right, she has to turn the paper, or *she* may turn and go around her drawing, just as she must turn in order to see the two rows of houses. If we wish to appreciate her painting, we have only to fold it along the base lines, and both rows of houses appear upright. This ingenious expression of "both sides" is not uncommon among children's creative concepts. But much more common are the "slanted" chimneys drawn at an angle toward the roof, or the slanted trees or houses on a mountain. The origin of both these expressions is the same. A mountain goes first up and then down. For the child, the feeling for movement is much more important than how the mountain "looks." Certainly the line can express movement much better than any other art form. We move along a line; the flying ball flies in a "curved line"; the shooting arrow flies along a line. If we move up a mountain, a line turning upward will best express this movement to the child. If we go downward, the line moves downward, too. However, let us imagine that the line is a piece of wire, and that the houses, trees, and so on, are attached to it. If the wire "moves up," the houses and trees fastened to the wire slant in the same fashion that the child draws them. If the wire with the attached trees were to be bent on the top so as to indicate its downward trend, the houses would necessarily stand at an angle to it. The same is true of the chimneys on the roofs. "The roof moves up and down, and on it is the chimney."

Needless to say, the child does not think in terms of wires. They are only used to illustrate the child's mode of expression. The child, however, when climbing a mountain feels, "I am going upward; to my left is a tree," and he draws it as though he were going through a similar experience. He draws the mountain line going upward, and as he draws the tree to the left he draws it at a correct angle.

Since this type of expression originates in the child's own thinking and experience, any adult interference would only be disturbing to the child. It is for the parent to adjust to the child's thinking and enjoy the originality of his expression. To impose adult standards by criticizing the child's work as being drawn "upside down" would not only be indicative of a complete lack of understanding, but it would also discourage the child in his mode of expression (Fig. 39).

39 "Children on the Playground." Look at the children forming a circle. (See page 116) (From "Creative and Mental Growth," Revised Ed.)

41 My child always uses the same color for the same object. The color of the sky remains blue even when it rains. (See page 118) (From "Creative and Mental Growth," Revised Ed.)

MY CHILD OFTEN DRAWS A HOUSE AS IF YOU COULD SEE
THE ROOMS THROUGH THE WALLS

Mary broke her ankle. She was brought, on a stretcher, by ambulance to the hospital. The pain was not great enough to deprive her of her important experiences. First she was taken to the X-ray department, then through a long hall to the dressing room, where her ankle was bandaged, and from there on a bed with rollers to the elevator and up to the third floor, to the children's ward. When Mary came home, she drew the whole hospital, or the parts which were important to her—the entrance, the X-ray room, the long hall through which she enjoyed rolling, the room where her ankle was bandaged, the elevator, and finally her bed in the children's ward. All this she included in her painting. A hospital would be just another house for her if it

40   The inside is as important as the outside (X-ray picture). (See page 118)

did not include all her important experiences. That she drew the floors as though the hospital walls were transparent was her logical method of expression.

Children at this level of development do not distinguish between external reality and their own emotional reaction. Regardless of what is possible in reality, they express what is significant to them. If the inside of an object is emotionally as important as the outside, children include both in their creative expression. If only the outside is significant, the outside is drawn. If, however, the inside is of special meaning to them, their painting will show the inside only. (Fig. 40)

MY CHILD ALWAYS USES THE SAME COLORS FOR THE SAME OBJECTS

Some children discover the relationship between objects and color earlier than others. Whenever they discover that the sky is blue, a lawn green, or a roof red, they will be proud of their discovery (Fig. 41). They would also like to be sure of their achievement. As we have seen, whenever a child wants to gain confidence in a newly discovered concept, he gains it by repeating it; in this case, repeating the same colors for the same object. These repetitions do not mean stiffness or rigidity. On the contrary, they indicate the discovery of a new experience and the enjoyment of mastery. This kind of repetition is not repetition for repetition's sake. The child does not repeat the same green lawn again and again. He uses different lawns whenever his experiences provide for them. However, he will always paint them the same green color, since this is the color which he originally established for a lawn. The color belongs to a lawn just as the sun belongs to the sky. He will even paint the lawn green, when actually it is brown. Such an established relationship between color and object will not change unless a definite emotional experience induces a deviation. For instance, a child may always paint the foliage of a tree green. It was green at the time the child first saw it, when he established the relationship between foliage and color. Now fall has come and, assuming that the child remains in this stage of development, he will continue to use his established color, disregarding the turning colors of the foliage or even the bare trees. If the child, however, has had an experience of emotional significance with the turned colors—perhaps on a walk or by collecting leaves of vivid fall colors—he will change his established color relationships.

To motivate our children in establishing more sensitive color relationships is a very important task. Let the child discover his own relationships by having him "search for color." However, never insist on "realistic" color relationships, or on imposing your adult sense of color. The child must be given the freedom of discovering his relationships of colors to objects and of expressing them independent of adult impositions. Each child has his own highly individualized color relationships based upon fundamental first experiences.

MY CHILD NEVER MIXES PAINT

Most children at this level of development are so absorbed in the establishment of a relationship between color and object that the quality of the relationship does not matter. One day Mary discovers that the lawn is green and that she can also paint it green in her painting. This discovery absorbs her emotionally so much that she neither cares whether the green is a yellowish or a bluish green, nor is she interested in it. Since the desire to mix colors grows only out of the need to express finer distinctions and differences, it is quite natural for the child not to mix her paint. Only when Mary becomes interested in distinguishing between lawns, or when she starts to see the finer differences in color, will she also start to mix her paint.

We have distinguished between Mary's "interest" in the lawn and her ability to see and observe finer differences in color. Interests may be of emotional or intellectual origin. Mary may become interested in her lawn because she helped seed it and now is waiting for its growth. But she may also have developed an interest in different types of lawns, one being more bluish green, while another may be more of a yellowish shade. Her knowledge of different lawns, as well as her emotional interest in watching their growth, may determine a more differentiated color relationship. It is this understanding and emotional interest which we must foster in order to make our children more sensitive to color.

Very rarely do children develop the ability visually to observe the finer qualities and distinctions of colors at this age level. Visual observations usually set in later, when the child becomes more critical of his environment. Do not force your child to observe things. Observation is an ability which develops. If the need for observation is not present, the child may only become critical toward his environment without improving his power of observation. This self-awareness caused by a premature critical attitude will only make the child adult-like, and thereby reduce his unconscious creative responses. Too many parents still think that art consists of depicting nature, and that "correct" color relationships are a part of it. It cannot be emphasized enough that the child's free and flexible growth is more important than all the finished products which may please parents but harm the child.

To be sure, any natural emotional reaction toward color on your part will influence the child in his sensitivity. I remember still with exaltation how my mother spoke of the beautiful colors around her. My feelings, if I remember correctly, were mere feelings of enjoyment and participation in her moving excitement. This coincides completely with the understanding of the child's development toward color as obtained by latest experiments. Yet I am sure that such emotional participation was an important incentive in my developing sensitivity toward color. Emotional reactions are, however, quite different from impositions. Let the child have freedom in his reactions, and let him find out for himself what he can discover in color relationships. This freedom is an essential part of growth in general, not merely growth in color perception.

MY CHILD PAINTS OR DRAWS VERY SMALL, USING
ONLY A SMALL PORTION OF THE PAPER

A child, if he has not had the possibility to create freely, cannot enjoy the entire area on the paper, in just the same way that one who has never been used to freedom cannot adequately use and enjoy it. If a child continually uses only a small portion of the paper for his paintings, the most logical immediate step may be to give him a smaller sheet of paper (Fig. 42a). He may find more security on it, for he will not have the feeling of being lost, as he obviously does on a large sheet. It is the same feeling some people have who have lived in a small room for a long time and suddenly move into a large hall where they lose their intimate relationships. They will feel lost in it, and as a substitute for the small room often establish themselves in a corner. There they feel more at home, better protected. The same is true for a child who feels "lost" on a large sheet of paper, and therefore "withdraws" into one

42a   My child paints or draws very small, using only a small portion of the paper.

42b   A drawing of the same child after effective motivation.   (See page 123)

corner. While it is of definite advantage to the child to be able to spread over a large sheet of paper, in fact to adjust to any size, there is nothing wrong with a child who prefers to draw small things with minute details. We would make just as great a mistake by saying that only large paper should be used as by restricting children to small sheets. Children are different in their personalities, and while large paper usually allows more freedom, it may also be frustrating for the child who feels lost on it.

If a child, however, persistently draws small in comparison to the sheet of paper he uses, feelings of insecurity or lack of confidence may be responsible for it. To tell a child to draw large would only be an imposition in disregard of the child's emotional needs. The child may need more affection and appreciation of his own work. He may also need more sensitive and flexible relationships to his environment, which may result in a greater consciousness of details. This in turn will create a more meaningful relationship to his work.

There is, however, another very important point for parents. We all know what a very important role economy plays in our lives. Yet we always think of economy in terms of money. How well can we get along with what we have? How can we most efficiently use what we have? These are our daily questions. It may never have occurred to us that economy in its spiritual meaning is one of the most important principles in art. "How can I express the best with the least?" Theoretically, in a work of art there should not be a superfluous brushstroke; everything should be where it is supposed to be. No change should be possible without changing the whole. When Mary is confronted with expressing her feelings and ideas on paper of a definite size, she is unconsciously faced with similar questions. "Where should I put the house, the fence, my dog, our big tree, the bench, the table?" All this needs to be organized. Some children have this feeling for organization within them. It is actually a feeling for the most economical use of the space they have at their disposal. Other children, however, do not care for the over-all use of the paper and the distribution of their representation over the whole area. This "organization," unconscious as it may be, is not only a vital part of art, but also of the child's whole personality.

The question arises: How can we influence this ability for organization in our children? Certainly we distinguish between rigid order and creative organization. Rigid order can be taught or even imposed. It is the type of order which is repeated again and again in filing letters alphabetically, in keeping a room "in order." Important as these activities are, they do not imply creative imagination or the involvement of the individual. The type of organization which is necessary for creative activity involves the whole individual, his thinking, feeling, and perceiving. In fact, when Johnny and Mary are able to integrate their feeling with their thinking and express it in their painting, they have already done a good bit of organization. If Mary does it only in a corner of her paper, it may indicate that she needs some help from you. The best help you can give her is to first discuss with her what she wants to express. If the use of only a fraction of the paper is due to lack of organization, she may be too impulsive in her approach, wrapped up in her thoughts without actually seeing the sheet of paper. To discuss her creative intentions might give you a good opportunity to insert such questions as: "Mary, you spoke of a river. Let us think it over, where is this river going to be? You said there was a house on one side of the river. On which side will it be?" Such questions will give the child some preliminary time before the organization of her subject matter takes place on paper. Of course, it is important, in talking to the child, not to tell her where to put things, or to criticize her poor distribution. Remember that the child grows only through her own experiences, and that imposition will only teach rigid order, and not a feeling for creative organization (Fig. 42b).

MY CHILD WANTS EVERYTHING TO LOOK "REAL"

Since the concept of art in which objects appear realistically is a typical adult concept, we have to be extremely careful in accepting the desire of the young child for realism as a desire of his own. In most cases such a desire has been imposed on the child by false criticism. If the child's confidence in his creative abilities has been shaken by criticism which made him aware of his inability to compete with nature, he will from then on ask for help in his desire to draw "naturally." Only in very rare cases is such a desire in young children genuine. Since it normally goes hand in hand with the child's great desire for observation and visual discoveries, it can easily be detected. If your child, out of his own urge, often sits in front of nature, observes details in the landscape, remarks about them and feels obviously drawn to nature, his desire for realistic representation may be genuine. In this rare case he may need more than your help; he may need the proper guidance of a sympathetic art teacher.

If your child, however, is not genuinely interested in nature, and only wants to draw "photographically," two important points have to be considered by parents. The first point deals with our concept of art, and the second with the meaning of art for your child.

To begin with, we should know that art never has been a true representation of objects, but an expression of our personal vision. Ever since art existed, art has been the expression of our experiences with things. The representation of an object exactly as it is, is not art. If this were art, the artist would be completely excluded; because if ten different individuals were to make an exact representation of the same object, the final result would be the same. A work of art is an expression of human feelings and ideas. If ten artists were to express their feelings and ideas about an object, they would all achieve different results according to their different relationships to the object and the feeling they have established for it. Let us pretend that ten artists want to express the sea. One may be impressed by its vastness, because he can look out over the sea for great distances; the second by the continuous, never ending motions of the waves; the third by the textures of the sea plants washed ashore; the fourth by the noise of the tossing waves; the fifth by the mist and spray in the air, and so forth. Each artist would use *his* basic experience and would express it in *his own* way. If distance and depth were the motivating factors, the artist might emphasize the horizon in its distant quality, and nothing else but water and sky; if the motion of the waves was the inspiration, a rhythmic expression of the type of movement experienced might be the result; if the texture of the sea plants motivated the artist, a design of sea-plant textures might be the final outcome. In many instances the desire for photographic representation is then only an escape from facing one's own experiences. This is especially true for the child between 7 and 10 years who has not yet become aware of his realistic environment.

The other question which we should always keep before us deals with the meaning which art has for our children. Let us never forget, *never*, that *our* taste must not guide the child's art expression. Whatever the final product may be, if the child has profited by it in his experiences and growth, it is more important to the child than any final product which pleases us but has interfered with his growth. Only when the child faces his *own* experiences in his art will he apply himself to them and grow with them. If he does not face his *own* experiences, but experiences which are imposed upon him and therefore are inconceivable to him—like perspective: the ability to express distance, depth, and the three-dimensional quality of objects—the child will only be frustrated.

What then should we do when Johnny says, "But it does not look real." The simplest answer is: "But Johnny, it does not need to look 'real'; there are many paintings which do not look real." If Johnny is satisfied, then all he needs is some kind of confirmation. But if he is persistent and says, "But I want it to look real," it is up to us to find out why he wants it to look "real." As has been said before, if his desire goes hand in hand with his power for observation he may be the child who needs some "technical help" from an art specialist. In most instances, however, you will find that the child can easily be "diverted" from his false realistic intentions by simply asking him, "But Johnny, what do you want to paint?" In most cases your child will answer, "A house, a dog, a figure." This would be a clear indication that a house, a dog, or a figure has not become a personal experience of your child. Therefore, from now on you should be very anxious to make it a personal experience in which your child becomes personally involved. "Which house do you want to paint? Do you mean our house? When it was raining hard, as it was last week, when you left for school in your

43 Children may use either hand for painting.

new raincoat?" Any such motivation would focus your child's attention on a definite situation in which the "realistic" attitude becomes
subordinate to the child's specific experience. The child may still need
a more detailed discussion to overcome his inhibitions, such as: "How
many floors has our house? Which is your room? When you leave the
house, do you have to go over steps?" Such questions will involve the
child still more in an experience which is *his*. Soon he will forget that
he wanted to draw "a house that looks real." It will be much more important to him that it is really raining hard. Needless to say, your praise,
for whatever he has achieved, will be very important in this situation.*

MY CHILD PAINTS AIMLESSLY

Let us first consider what we call "aimlessly." A parent once said that
her child painted aimlessly because she had not been given "direction."
This, of course, we should not call aimless, because we assume that the
child should develop his own direction for his creative work and that
the teacher in school or the parent at home will only support the child
in *his* creative activity. If we speak of "aimless" painting, we refer to the
child's lack of intention. If we ask Virginia, "What are you painting?"
and Virginia answers, "I don't know; just something," needless to say
Virginia has the right just to dabble in paint, or merely to experiment
and wait for the outcome. If she does this now and then, I should not
call her attitude toward her work "aimless." If, however, she continuously dabbles aimlessly or answers that she just paints "something," it is
a sign that she cannot concentrate on an experience which was important enough to her that she can aim at it. Obviously, this is not a lack
of ability which refers to creative activity only. It is a difficulty which
is part of her personality. The question occurs whether creative activity
can be helpful to her in her ability to concentrate on a definite task.

The greater the urge for expression in the child, the more will he concentrate on his work. The urge for expression, however, is present only
if an experience is strong enough to promote expression. An experience
is strong enough only if it affects the child in his basic needs, and this
will be true only if he is sensitive to his basic needs. By the term "basic
needs" we understand here only the needs which are basic to his emo-

* See "The Correct Motivation for My Child's Creative Work," page 27.

tional and mental well-being, mainly the environmental conditions which include the love and affection to which every child is entitled.

The question then reverts to us parents. Do we give our child enough attention, or do we let him wander aimlessly about? If he wanders aimlessly about, we should not be surprised that his art expression shows the same attitude. The only cure for our child is for us to change our relationship to him, to give him more attention, discuss with him what he has on his mind, and appreciate any attempt on his part to concentrate on one experience.

This may be difficult in the beginning. During this period storytelling hours, games, or discussions about things in which your child is particularly interested are suggested. Creative expression in the form of painting or drawing is not important during this initial period. Actually, this "warming-up" time is for the purpose of reinforcing your child's confidence in you, and to give him an opportunity to collect his experiences and "learn" to concentrate at a definite time on a definite experience. It is of great significance that you are aware of your task of providing your child with situations which make him more sensitive toward his environment. By "sensitive" we mean more apprehensive to emotional, perceptual (experiences referring to seeing, hearing, touch and movement) and social experiences.

From what has been said, it is obvious that forcing a child to concentrate or aim at something definite would only create harmful reactions. To introduce a "creative hour" by enforcing it on the child may cause him to develop an aversion toward creative activity. By that, we mean that we should not "make" the child "create" when his mind is elsewhere. Creative expression develops only out of the child's own urge for it. The more secure the child feels in his own thinking and feeling, the less will he be "aimless" in his creative work. It is up to you to provide him with that security.

MY CHILD HATES CLAY

If a child does not develop the proper feeling toward certain forms of expression or materials, it may be owing to bad experiences in the past with similar material. It may also be caused by the difficulty which this medium provides for the expression of his particular concepts.

A child may have unpleasant memories of clay that is too wet and sticky. From then on, he "hates" clay. But a child may also want to include environment or color in his creative concept. Since he cannot do it in clay, he "hates" clay.

It is important for us to find out which of the two reasons influenced the child in his reaction. If it is merely the unpleasant memory, it will not be difficult to help the child to get rid of his aversion. The simplest way is not to use clay, but plasticine or synthetic plastic materials recently placed on the market. They do not have sticky consistency. It is also often very helpful to begin by modeling with the child. You do not need to finish a product; simply engage in kneading or forming the plastic material. Never force a child to use creative media. After a few trials the child will have fun in experimenting with the new material. Once he enjoys modeling in a plastic material, he can easily be converted to clay. Again, it is the urge for expression which makes him overcome his difficulty.

However, if your child does not like to express himself in clay because he finds that it restricts his creative ideas, there is no need for him to model. Clay is merely another medium which, as has been pointed out, adds many possibilities for the child's expression and growth. If for some good reason the child prefers another form of expression that better serves his growth, there is no reason why he should continue to use a material with which he cannot adequately express himself.

MY CHILD LOVES CLAY AND DOES NOT WANT TO PAINT

It may occur that your child loves clay and does not care to paint. If this love is a genuine one, clay will adequately serve as a means of expression. The reason for such preference may be found in the fact that some individuals, children and adults, express themselves more easily in terms of what they feel through their bodies, through their motions and emotions. For this they do not need environment. In fact it may only be disturbing to them. Johnny wants to express anger. For that he does not need environment. He feels that his anger is best expressed by modeling just his head. He also loves the feeling when he runs, when he lifts a heavy load, or when he sits and contemplates. All this, he can best express in clay. There is nothing wrong in this, except that Johnny may not adequately develop his feeling for his environment. It is for this reason that we should now and then try to stimulate his creative thinking toward environmental experiences. We can do so by using his modeling as a starting point. If Johnny has modeled himself thinking with his head supported by his hands, we can ask him: "Johnny, where were you thinking? In your room? At the window?" If you encourage his environmental thinking, he may one day start to paint on his own initiative. You may encourage this step by making remarks which may be conducive to the atmosphere of painting, such as, "I could imagine a painting of you sitting near the window." But by no means force him to paint, or impose your image on him. He will paint if he feels the need. If he does not, neither your encouragement nor an authoritarian attitude will help him in his growth. It may only make his aversion stronger.

You may, however, help him in his urge to express himself with clay.

The most important help you can give him is to assist him in establishing a greater sensitivity in his body feelings. "Johnny, when you were thinking hard, where did you feel it? When you were holding your head, which part of your head was in your hands? When you supported your head, where was your elbow? Did you sit upright?" Such questions would increase his sensitivity toward his body feelings and would encourage him to establish more sensitive relationships between himself and his clay work.

44 Children love to model in clay.

WHAT MATERIAL SHALL I BUY?

In the use of materials, not much has changed. Because your child may still want to use his crayons or chalks occasionally, he should be allowed to keep a set of each. Thick crayons are still preferred to the thin ones, and he still does not need a large set. In fact, he will never need it, since a large set only discourages the mixing of colors. He should also have his poster paint. It no longer needs to be thick. We can also gradually depart from the absorbent paper and give him "easel paper" or white wrapping paper. Sometimes he may prefer brown or neutral-colored paper, using white as an additional color. He may want to use his hair brush more than his bristle brush, because he may feel the need for greater detail, which can be more easily handled with the hair brush. Now and then your child may want to put more water into the paint to find out how colors may be mixed by the merging quality of watery paint.

Your child would also like to have his plastic bag filled with clay or plasticine. His box with scrap material has given him many hours of great enjoyment, and he should continue to collect more scraps. As he grows, he may have even more fun in building all kinds of constructions.

the 10-12 year old:
an important word to parents

DURING these years your child will go through very important and, for his future, decisive stages in his development. In the beginning he will discover the fact that he can have real friends. He will also find that he can be socially independent, even if this is done in a romantic way in his group. He will discover that he is more powerful in a group than he is alone, and by virtue of this he will explore the possibilities of cooperation. Many parents look at these years of development as awkward and undesirable years. The child does not want to stay at home; he likes to be with his friends. Children get all kinds of ideas for which their parents are not ready. Johnny wants to sleep outdoors; he wants to take hikes overnight. Mary has her group too, with whom she closely associates. These are important stages in the development of our children. We can only understand them if we try to put ourselves in their place. Let us imagine that we never knew what "friendship" meant, friendship on an equal basis. Let us also imagine that one day we discover that certain ties develop between us and another person, ties which we have never felt before. We also discover that we have the same interests as the other person and that we can do things together. In so doing, we discover that some things can be more easily done together than alone. All these are very fundamental discoveries. They are of extreme importance because they influence not only our lives but also the lives of our neighbors, for friendships consist of teamwork. During this important period of his development your child actually lays the ground for his ability to work in groups and to cooperate.

It is then of the utmost importance for you to foster all activities which promote your child's desire and needs for group participation.

what happens if I do not respect the child's desire to have friends or to associate with groups?

THE word "gang" has a somewhat bitter taste in our society. Yet we have seen of what importance group life is for the development of your child. The urge for social independence during this period is as fundamental as cooperation is for his future.

If we suppress this very natural tendency in the growth of our children, we interfere with one of the most important character trends. The outcome of such interference is a hostile attitude, the forming of groups in secret, or both. The hostile attitude of such groups is usually seen in their destructive character. It is, however, usually forgotten that the basic cause of these tendencies lies in the lack of love and the inability of parents to see the needs of their children. It is not by accident that juvenile delinquency reaches its peak during this stage of development. It must also be remembered that at this age level our children are still children. This means that they neither control their actions nor think and plan with the awareness of adults. Their actions are usually guided merely by instinctive drives. This makes their destructive tendencies even more dangerous. A child has no consideration for the future effects of his action.

The fundamental reason why we should help our children during this stage of development should be determined by the importance of co-operation, the meaning of social interaction and group work. Even by sacrificing some of our own comfort we should provide the child with opportunies to experience his social needs. It is not the same for the child to be surrounded by adults, even if the adults think that they are very sympathetic to him. I have heard parents say, even with some resent-ment, that they feel that their child is given enough opportunity for cooperation at home, and that they take their child out for hikes and that the father "even goes fishing with Johnny." As important as family life is, we have to consider that Johnny is growing, and not every kind of experience can be obtained within the family. In fact, family ties and family life will gain from the experiences which Johnny has had with groups of his age. If Johnny has confidence in you, he will tell you of his experiences, whether they are with the Cub Scouts, in school, with church organizations, or with a group of his own.

THE MEANING OF GROUP WORK

In the light of what has been said, group work as a means of pro-moting social interaction will easily be understood. In particular, if we think of creative group activity, the fact that a whole group is carried by one "creative motive" will greatly increase the desire for group par-ticipation and cooperative attitude. However, group work is only effec-tive if the single child has the feeling that he could not have accom-plished what the whole group could do. For instance: Johnny, Virginia, and Mary meet in your home and would like to work on a common painting. Of course, the paper has to be of good size. For this purpose we get a small roll of brown craft paper. We spread it either on the floor or, if we can, tack it on the wall. Johnny, Virginia, and Mary are of different temperaments. It may happen that they interfere with each other, especially if Mary thinks that Virginia is spoiling her concept, or if Johnny has the feeling that he could have done better by himself.

In order to avoid such discouragements, some initial guidance on your part is suggested. Needless to say, the less your guidance is felt by the children, the better it is for them. That is why it is of great advantage for adults to remain in the background as much as possible. For initial interference to be kept to a minimum, it is suggested that a material be chosen in which each child can work separately on his own, but which also lends itself to assembly purposes. A group of children decided to work on a harbor using the technique of paper cutting. Any five-and-ten-cent store usually has a supply of assorted colored paper. Each child cut out his own boat. Since the work was done in a coastal area, the children were very boat-minded. One cut out at sailboat, another a destroyer, a fishing boat, rowboats, motorboats, steamships, and even a ferry. Every one of the children tried to compete with the others in making more and better boats. Such natural competition was not only wholesome for the children but made them aware of the contributions of the others. Finally a large number of boats were cut out. Now they had to decide where to put all the boats. They had a big piece of cardboard on which they painted the docks and the water. All the boats were pasted according to a mutual arrangement. It was a grand harbor. Each child had boats that looked much better in the group than by themselves. Each child had the feeling that he could not have accomplished

45 In group work they learn to cooperate.

such a big task alone. Surely this helped greatly to increase the feeling for cooperation.

If the children have become used to the effectiveness of group work and cooperation, they will no longer interfere with one another even by painting together on a large painting. They will agree on the areas which each has decided to select. However, only such topics should be chosen which are related to group experiences, such as, "We are at a country fair" or "We are at the zoo." In this case one child can paint a merry-go-round, another a shooting gallery, a third a puppet show, and so on. Since all deal with the same topic, it will give them an excellent opportunity to discuss questions of mutual importance.

If the child feels his importance, if opportunities are given to him to work and play with his companions, if he finds emotional outlets to express what he has on his mind, if his "gang" or group is regarded by you as a social unit, and therefore respected, he will not only regard you as a parent but also as his understanding friend.

"CREATIVE AFTERNOONS" WITH FRIENDS

Soon, such an occasion may become a very desirable custom. It all depends on you. The more you want to be a part of it, the less will the children be attracted by it. Don't feel hurt about it; children at this age do not like to include adults in their affairs. Your fun may be in helping your child plan for it, in supporting it, and above all in the fact that you see your child cooperate with the group.

Do not think that creative activity consists of painting and drawing only. Anything which motivates your child in solving a problem originally and independently will contribute to his creative growth. If you have a back yard and supply your child with some old boards or building material, you have provided him with a very stimulating art material. Soon you will see the whole group planning to build with the "treasures" you gave them. But do not forget that planning is already an important part of the feeling of social independence, which your child is yearning for. Of course they are going to build a "hide-out." If you do not have a back yard, the basement, or even a room, may be used as a substitute. Building is one of the most desirable and useful occupations during this period, because it lends itself best to group participation. Once the hide-out is built, all kinds of other attractions can be

46 A "Creative Afternoon."

added. Above all, from then on the "Creative Afternoons" can be continued there. Useful objects of clay or other materials can be made. The child, being more aware of his environment, will quickly develop the desire to make the place more attractive. A simple bench may be built, and a table added. Remember that these self-made, primitive-looking pieces of furniture mean more to your child than the most beautiful bought furniture. Girls might want to add some curtains, or they might want to do some cooking on an outdoor stove, for cooking, too, is creative as long as it is experimental and inventive. Children can have a wonderful time if you leave them to themselves.

If everything has to be done indoors, and if nothing else but the "creative corner" is at the disposal of your child, many other types of

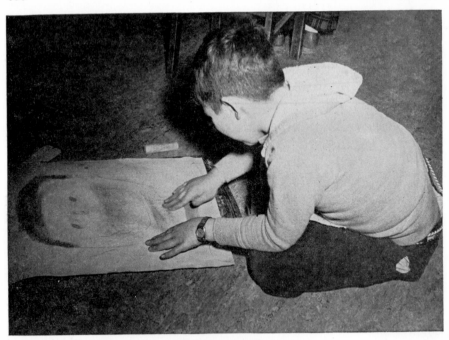

47 Painting on the floor has great advantages.

creative group work can be initiated. Besides the previously described paper cutting and assembling of a common picture, the building of good-sized models is always fun. A Wonderland, a farm, a circus, a village, a department store, are excellent projects. Whenever such a project is started, a good scrap box with wires, screens, stoppers, wood, foils, pipe cleaners, cardboard, tacks, Scotch tape, and so on, should be available. Paste, paint, and clay are also necessary materials. Here, too, the planning of how to attack the project constitutes an important initial step. It is the "warming-up" period in which children exchange their thoughts and learn to agree, to reason or to disagree and find new approaches. What goes into a Wonderland? This can be attacked simultaneously by all, by first building one fantastic wondertree, then a wonderflower, or by adopting other suggestions coming from the children; or it can be done in separate projects where each child selects a form to create. If all these separate projects are assembled into a final project, a higher group consciousness may result.

If a village is built, each of the children selects his part. It is needless to say that materials should be used that best serve the imagination of the child. A little piece of window screen can do wonders. It can become the fence around a house and it can be used as the basis to "plaster" a

48a   The whole group is carried by one "creative motive."

48b   Children discuss a mural project on one of their "Creative Afternoons."
(See page 135)   Courtesy of Art Association, Montreal, Canada.

wall. Needless to say, creatively free children develop more ingenuity in their work. The great advantage of group work also lies in the fact that those who are usually inflexible in their thinking may become inspired by the rest of the group. "Natural competition," the type of competition which grows out of group participation, is a very healthy incentive of group work. No rewards but the feeling of each individual that he would like to contribute his best to the enterprise of the group are necessary for such competition. His "best," however, is usually inspired by growing standards which intermittently are determined by the different members of the group. Johnny cuts a beautiful house out of plaster and uses many materials ingeniously on it. Mary becomes inspired by it and thinks of a still more ingenious use. Johnny, inspired by Mary, goes on inventing. This type of natural competition is like a chain reaction.

It is very important that "Creative Afternoons" be well organized, for children easily lose themselves in "social doodling," that is, in senseless back-and-forth talking or teasing. This happens especially if there is no "group-leader" among them who starts to organize. It is at this point that you as a parent can contribute most. In most instances it would be enough if you place the proper material before the children. A little preliminary discussion with your child—"What do you want to do today?"—would be helpful. If your child is indifferent to this question, a few suggestions may induce a more positive attitude. Often such a suggestion as, "Do you think you girls would like to use your cooking utensils?" or, "Do you want to have the scrap box on the table?" is enough to stimulate activity. Sometimes a topic may be suggested, "How about making animals out of pipe cleaners today to see what everyone can do?" or, "Let's all make a circus today." However, once the "crowd" is assembled, you should remain in the background. If you can make "Creative Afternoons" a weekly occasion, you will provide your child with an invaluable source for experiences so badly needed at a period where he has to assure himself of his social independence.

MY CHILD SEEMS TO EMPHASIZE THE DIFFERENCE BETWEEN BOYS AND GIRLS IN HIS PAINTINGS AND OTHERWISE

When children discover their interest in groups, their first real friendships, they also discover that girls have different interests than boys. This is particularly true of the society in which we live. If this tendency is not guided into constructive channels, as has been suggested in "Creative Afternoons," of mixed groups or other coeducational occasions, boys and girls alike will start the well known "secret societies" into which only girls or only boys are accepted. From that it is not far to starting "wars" against each other in which boys and girls alike, by feeling attracted to each other, choose to give this beginning attraction a contrary expression because they are incapable of adequately dealing with their newly awakened interest and feeling (Figs. 49b and 49c).

49a   Children dress for a pageant in costumes which they have made themselves.
(See page 136)   Courtesy of Art Association, Montreal, Canada.

49b   My child is now interested in characterizing boys and girls. (See page 141)   Courtesy Chicago Public Schools.

49c   My child is interested in dresses. Courtesy Chicago Public Schools.

The less opportunity your child has to engage in natural coeducational situations, in play, in creative activities, in group work, or other social occasions, the more will he emphasize the difference between the sexes. Secret talks, the usual teasing, and other destructive tendencies are usually only the result of frustrated feelings. Of course, it *is* natural for children of this age to become more aware of themselves, their own power, and their own social status. As a part of this awareness, it is also natural that boys develop a greater interest in girls, and vice versa. The attempt to suppress this interest would only increase its intensity.

One way in which this interest finds a natural form of expression is in the drawings and paintings of children of this age. The more this interest has been suppressed, the more will it come out in creative work. Thus, we usually see in the drawings and paintings of this period of development an emphasis on the characteristics of the different sexes, such as hair, fingernails, red lips, and dresses on girls, and mustaches, pants, uniforms, and other characteristics on boys. Thus, creative activity serves as a kind of balance in newly discovered interest for the other sex. Needless to say, the wise parent will only support this interest by promoting gatherings in which both boys and girls get used to each other and work and play together under natural conditions.

MY CHILD'S PAINTINGS APPEAR "STIFF"

In characterizing boys as boys and girls as girls in his art work, the child may easily become tied up with certain details. Since particulars of dress are very important to your child during this period of his development, he may concentrate so much on them that he loses connection with the rest of his painting. We, too, often lose connection with the whole if we become interested in details. Has it not occurred to you that you became so attracted by a brooch on a friend's blouse that you cannot remember the dress she wore? Similarly, when the child concentrates on meaningful details he may easily lose the feeling for motion, and his paintings appear stiff. This stiffness may be seen not only in figures but also in the relationships between figures and objects. This is only natural when it occurs in the presence of a greater emphasis on details.

If, however, stiffness occurs in the absence of a greater concentration on details, it may have a different meaning. First, let us describe what we understand by stiffness. By "stiffness" we understand the inability of the child to relate figures and objects to each other. In many cases this occurs in children who have either no apparent desire for cooperation or are frustrated in their discovery of social independence. Just as they feel isolated themselves, they apparently express this feeling of detachment in their creative work. While this may only be temporary, and soon outgrown, it is suggested that some attention be paid to it.

It is quite obvious that in order to achieve better relations in his painting, personality changes within the child are necessary. It would therefore be entirely wrong to attack the problem superficially and show the child "how to relate his figures" to one another in his paintings. Such actions would only mean betraying ourselves by not helping the child in his difficulties.

MY CHILD NOW PAINTS THE SKY DOWN TO THE "HORIZON"

As the child becomes more aware of himself, he also becomes increasingly conscious of his environment. The feeling for environment becomes much more intense when environment has become meaningful. As long as the child is well taken care of by his parents and is not aware of his social potentialities in a group of his own, environment is only meaningful if he relates it to his immediate self. When he starts to associate with his group and begins to make discoveries, he feels suddenly surrounded by an environment which no longer expresses merely his own feeling, such as "The sky is above, the ground is below, and in between is the air." A painting with a strip of air above, a base line below, and in between nothing no longer satisfies his needs. He walks with his group across the streets, in the woods and fields and sees the sky meeting the line of the earth (Fig. 50). His newly acquired awareness will express itself in his new spatial concept.

50 **My child now paints the sky down to the horizon.** Courtesy Chicago Public Schools.

MY CHILD DOES NOT WANT TO ASSOCIATE WITH THE OTHER SEX

Once children have become aware of the differences in the interests of boys and girls, we often find that, *when not given enough opportunity for natural relationships,* hostile feelings develop. It is here that creative activities can be most beneficial. Almost as a rule, boys look down at girls, and vice versa. In school they separate voluntarily. In fact, when Johnny hears that girls are invited to a gathering, he prefers to stay at home or go out with *his* friends. Mary thinks that what boys are doing is silly. Therefore, she does not want to participate in any project or group where boys are present.

It is true that in many cases girls of this age are more advanced in their development than boys. However, this is not the question; we are not discussing whether boys and girls of the same age should be together. It does not matter if the boys are older than the girls. It is, however, important that both develop a feeling for cooperation, regardless of their sex.

Temporary feelings of animosity are quite natural as a part of the group consciousness which develops during this period. It is, however, important that such feelings do not become deeply rooted. To avoid this, our children must first be able to free themselves of any aggressive feeling which they may have against the other sex. Here art can make a major contribution. If Johnny does not want to associate with girls, it would be very good for him to draw and paint them. In his paintings he should find ample opportunity to express his negative feelings if he desires, and in this way provide for more constructive relationships. Naturally, this method may not always be successful, but it is of great importance that he be provided with a kind of safety valve to let off steam which otherwise may easily lead to an explosion of a socially destructive feeling. In most instances, however, the child will grow out of this stage into a period where he will not only cooperate with adults but will be open to reasoning.

51   If your child has experienced friendships and group activities he will not only cooperate with adults but will be open to reasoning.   Courtesy Public Schools, Pittsburgh, Pa.

MY CHILD APPEARS HOSTILE TOWARD ADULTS

When adults interfere with the child's desire for social independence, with his "group life," the child, frustrated in his feelings, turns against the adult. It would appear very simple to prevent this from happening, by not interfering with the child. This, however, is extremely difficult, and almost impossible, for we feel responsible not only for the child's creative and mental growth but also for his physical well-being. Undoubtedly in the course of his development he will ask for things which are not only detrimental to his health but otherwise in disagreement with family life, the school, or our beliefs. He may ask to go on overnight hikes, yet the parent may feel the child is not yet ready to do this without someone being responsible. He may want to sleep outdoors with the children of his "gang," but you may find it too cold outside. He may prefer to be with *his* group just when you need him or want to be with him. There are all kinds of situations which may make your child believe that you are interfering with his "life." You may not even be aware of your child's attitude. For the child, however, you represent the adult. Therefore he may establish a hostile feeling not only toward you but toward all adults. This is quite commonly found during this period of development, and while it may lead to tensions it may not be of long duration. But since it always leaves some kind of imprint on the child's character and personality, we shall try to find ways by which we can keep the child's confidence and at the same time keep him in "acceptable" bounds.

The key to the solution probably lies in the interpretation of what you consider "acceptable." If you can sacrifice some of your comfort and stretch the acceptable as far as possible, your child will happily grow through this period of development. Go as far as you can in providing your child with proper opportunities to live and cooperate with his group. The more you do, the less will the child find the need for "more." Above all, have confidence in your child and let him settle his own affairs. Always remember that it is easier to prevent the development of hostile feelings than to deal with them after they have become a part of your child's emotional reactions.

In the creative activity of our children, we find countless opportunities to give expression to their hostile feelings, directly or indirectly. Under direct expression, we understand those in which either the topic or the kind of expression confronts the child with his feelings and thus provides for easier acceptance. We call indirect the type of expression which serves as an emotional outlet to the child but has no direct bearing on his thinking. Johnny may just have had a quarrel with his mother because he wanted to play with his friends on the lawn, but his mother thought the lawn too wet after a heavy rain. So Johnny takes one of the sticks which he keeps in his scrap box, and starts briskly to whittle it. First, probably aimlessly. However, after a while he calms down and gets more interested in whittling and produces a very startling piece of work. All of his accumulated feelings of hostility or frustration may have gone into the stick. He did not confront himself with his issue by drawing or painting a topic which had direct relationship to his hostility or frustration, but he used his activity unconsciously as an emotional outlet. Please, do not tell Johnny that it was better for him to whittle his stick. Indeed, it would have been better for him to have rubbers and play outside, even if it were wet. But it would have been still worse if he had had no creative corner to which he could withdraw and no scrap box from which to take a piece of wood. There are countless other cases which may need different reactions, cases which range from being well justified in abiding by our judgment to those where we fail to give the child the opportunity to discover his social independence. Most important, however, remains the fact of becoming aware of the great significance which this period of development has for the future of our child and his ability to cooperate. Once we are aware of the problem, we are likely to treat our children differently and avoid mistakes which otherwise we would not have recognized.

WHAT ART MATERIALS DOES MY CHILD NEED?

As the child grows, his desire for experimentation and the use of different materials grows. We have seen that group activities are most important during this period of development. For paper-cutting murals he will need assorted colored paper. A good pair of scissors is very important. His friends should bring their own scissors. He needs a jar of paste. You can buy it or prepare it yourself. A box of tongue depressors is very useful. Tongue depressors can be used for distributing paste, for taking paint out of the jars, and in making models and constructing "designs." You may want to buy water colors (see page 144) in addition to the show-card paint (poster paint) which he already has. He may need another hair brush No. 12 in addition to the bristle brushes he still has. Never use a paint brush for paste. A roll of craft paper (heavy wrapping paper) is important as the base for group painting and paper cutting. Your child still needs his plastic bag with clay for modeling. He should have a small bag with plaster, which he may, after it is properly mixed with water, pour into a cardboard box and form a cube. After it has set, he may want to carve it. He needs a good-sized scrap box with pieces of wire screens, different wires, scraps of wood, stoppers, buttons, fibers, textiles, corrugated cardboard, tin foil, colored cellophane, and whatever he may collect, such as bark, rocks, shells, driftwood, plants, feathers, or whatever attracts him. The collecting of scraps by itself has great educational possibilities. It makes him sensitive toward these materials, particularly to the products of nature, once he learns to enjoy collecting them. Perhaps one of the most important art materials during this period is a good-sized toolbox. Do not make the mistake of buying your child inferior tools. He is just beginning to learn to appreciate what he produces. Such beginning is always difficult. Don't buy too many tools of one kind. In real group cooperation one of the important tasks is getting along with what one has and using it most efficiently.

Remember again that a good "creative corner" with good storage facilities, such as shelves or drawers, will not only help your child to keep his things in place but will save much money by avoiding waste of materials.

the 12-14 year old:
before my child grows up

If you have given your child enough opportunities for group activities, if he has experienced real friendships, he enters a stage in which you can talk to him and reason about almost anything—so much so that you may often forget that he has not yet grown up. Bear in mind, however, that in his reactions he is still a child. It may happen that you are involved in a serious discussion. Yet in the next moment your child may pick up a stick from the ground and, pretending that it's a gun, shoot with it. The difference between children and adults can best be seen in the different ways they play. Children may play hide-and-seek with the same unawareness as that with which they zoom a pencil through the air, using it as an airplane while imitating its noise. Such unawareness is characteristic of children. Quite obviously their imagination transforms a stick into a gun, or a pencil into an airplane. All children use their imagination in an uninhibited way; if an adult were to do the same he would be considered insane. For an adult a pencil is a pencil, and its

52 Although your child has grown, he still plays and reacts like a child. (See page 151) (From "Creative and Mental Growth," Revised Ed.)

function is to write. In his art, too, as in his play, the child uses his imagination without control. The adult, however, in his play as well as in his activities, uses his imagination with awareness. In his play he usually has rules and aims. In his activities he looks at the final product critically and considers it the important outcome. The change, however, from the unconscious approach to that of critical awareness is one of the most important characteristics of the beginning of adolescence. Usually this change is introduced by physical changes in the body.

Many parents are completely unaware of the importance of these changes to their children. The more unexpectedly these changes occur, the greater is the shock they cause. Any change, however small it may be, necessitates some kind of adjustment. The more serious the changes are, the greater are the difficulties under which an adjustment takes place. Since the bodily changes in an individual bring about a greater awareness of his place in society, a reorientation to his environment takes place. No wonder that our children are seriously affected by them. It is by no means rare to meet one of our child's friends after three months' summer vacation and scarcely recognize him. He was a child who laughed freely, unaware of anyone's reactions. Now he looks "wooden," doesn't know what to do with his legs, steps embarrassedly from one foot to the other, and answers with a constantly changing voice. "John, how you have changed!" is our usual reaction, while his is still shorter, "Yes'm." Most often before this change takes place, children freely engage in creative activities, while afterward, too critical to accept their own work, they frequently lose their creativeness, unless the desire for it is motivated.

As has been said before, the more unexpectedly the changes occur, the greater are the difficulties in adjusting to them. The more gradually such changes take place, the less do we feel them. To make sudden changes appear gradual necessitates some conditioning. For instance, if you were told that you had to move out of your home tomorrow, quite apart from the physical strain, the circumstance that you must suddenly part from your friends and your home would cause a great emotional upset. If, however, you were to hear many weeks ahead that there was a possibility that you might move, and this possibility gradually became certainty, you would easily adjust to the new situation. Still, when it arises and you leave everything behind you, you cannot escape the effect of the change!

The same is true of changes during adolescence. If we gradually prepare our children for them, they will better adjust to them when they arrive. The period, however, during which this conditioning should take place is the period which precedes adolescence, the period which we are about to discuss. Needless to say, we shall only discuss the changes which affect the child's art activities and what we can do to help him to adjust to them. Since his art activities are a part of his personality, the adjustment in this realm may well influence his adjustment in general.

MY CHILD WANTS TO DRAW OR PAINT REALISTICALLY

During this period of growth, some of our children develop a great urge to draw or paint realistically, that is, photographically. Art, as we have said before, is not the representation of things, but the expression of the experience we have with them. If we support or even emphasize the simple drive for photographic representation, we will not only divert the child from creative expression, but we will also hinder the development of his imagination, his own originality in thinking. The realistic representation of nature will make the child dependent on this. I know many children or adolescents who cannot draw anything unless they have something in front of them. Actually, they have become so dependent on the actual object that they feel lost without it.

Yet the urge to paint realistically is a genuine urge, and we must respect it (Fig. 53a). However, we can do much to help our child not to become a slave to it. The child's overemphasis on realistic representation is an indication of his new discovery and awareness of his environment. This newness of his visual experience often overpowers the other creative qualities. The danger that his desire may not meet his expectation is great. His skills and techniques may be inadequate for representing what he sees "accurately." "This does not look like a real tree, or a good figure," are common remarks. To make a tree appear accurate may be a photographic aim, but it is not an artistic one. Therefore, without hurting our child, we should direct his attention to his experience with the tree. "Is it a stormy day? Is the tree shaken by the wind?" Such questions which refer to a definite experience rather than to the accurate representation will deflect attention from a mere photographic representation. "From which direction does the wind blow?" is a question which would relate his thinking to the desired reality, yet it would also necessitate the child's identification with the situation. We could apply the same motivation to almost everything. "What is your figure doing? Does he push a cart? Let's see whether he pushes hard." Such

53a My child wants to paint "realistically." (See page 152) Courtesy of Educational Project, Museum of Modern Art, New York.

questions would give your child an opportunity for realistic representation, yet allow him to be included in the experience. His attention would also be deflected from the "good figure" to a meaningful experience.

The more we emphasize both the experience and the child's ability to represent it, the more we shall lead the child from the uncontrolled childish art to the more aware expression of the adolescent. This process is a gradual one. Great care is necessary on the part of the parents not to impose their own all too common desires for realistic art on their children when the temptation is great to regard it as "their expression."

IS IT NECESSARY THAT MY CHILD DRAWS IN GOOD PROPORTIONS?

Great cultures throughout the history of men have shown that "good proportions," that is, naturalistic proportions, are not necessarily a part even of great art. In medieval art Christ is painted large in comparison to the apostles or the rest of the picture. Parts which seemed significant often were exaggerated in size. Since proportions were not used according to naturalistic measurements, even in great art, we can understand that it is by no means a necessity to apply them when art is used to help your child in his growth. Don't let your own taste be the deciding factor. The only one to determine whether realistic proportions are an important part of your child's art is your child himself. But he too may be influenced in his desire by many outside forces—criticism at home or in school, the conventionally accepted art forms, remarks by his friends, and many others. It will therefore be important to find out whether "good proportions" really serve the needs of your child, or whether they are imposed forms of expression. This is not difficult at all, and as a parent you can easily detect it. Remember that this is important because all imposed forms of expression restrict your child and do not allow the unfolding of *his* creative thinking, *his* art activity, and with it, his personality (Fig. 53b).

There are children who always, in their art and elsewhere, refer to their visual impressions. In their paintings they attempt to represent the things they see and observe. They usually feel like "spectators," being outside the situation. They are good observers. There are also children who always feel emotionally involved in their experience. They do not feel themselves spectators, and are not impressed by what they see but by what they feel. Visual experiences remain almost meaningless. They paint their experiences according to their subjective feelings.

If your child, in his behavior as well as in his paintings, shows a preference for visual experiences, if he usually feels like a spectator looking at things from the outside, "good proportions" are probably a necessary part of his expression. His sensitive desire for "good proportions" then becomes a longing which should be fulfilled. This urge to draw realistic proportions will contribute most to its fulfillment. Yet we can help our child, but not by showing him "good proportions." *He* must discover them as *his* experience. Good proportions can be motivated either by placing the self in relationship to other things, or by pure observation. "Johnny, look at this lower branch. Can you still reach it, when you stretch out your arms and hands? Get on your tip-toes! Now, can you reach it?" Such experiences strongly motivate size relationships. "Are you too tall to get through the door? How much higher is the door than you? Could Daddy go through it?" Such motivations can be intermittently used whenever there is occasion for them. They are not only of value for your child's painting: they are mainly of importance because they apparently satisfy the child's needs and give him greater

53b It is more important that the child expresses *his* experience than that he draws in "good proportions." (See page 154)

security. They also gradually prepare him for the period when he will look more critically at his final product. It would be entirely wrong to measure things to get their proportions. This would only make your child dependent on the yardstick, and whenever he could not actually measure he would feel lost. For the art of the visually-minded child, a yardstick or any instrument used for measuring is only a crutch. The more the child is exposed to real experiences which make him aware of proportions, the better will he be able to apply them freely.

If your child, however, becomes emotionally involved in his experiences, "good proportions" would only be a hindrance in his art expression. For him, sizes refer to *importance*, as they do in medieval and expressive art. When Mary holds something very precious in her hands, and she is afraid she might drop it, both her hands as well as the precious object may appear exaggerated in her painting. For her, this "proportion of value" is just as true as the visual proportion is for Johnny. It fulfills her need to express her experience. As we have given support to Johnny's desire for realistic proportions, we shall also appreciate and support Mary's need for her type of subjective proportions. "Mary, I know you felt that this was a very precious thing in your hands. I can see it in your painting. Mary, I see you are thinking hard. Where do you feel it most?" Here, too, the motivation does not need to refer to a creative work. The support which Mary gets through your ability to feel as she does encourages her desire for expression and gives her more security. It may be pointed out, especially to parents, that it is much more difficult for children who rely more on their own emotional interpretation to remain true to themselves, because the conventional appreciation of art is not on their side. This is one more reason why you must be careful not to harm their sensitive expression.

Thus, both realistic proportions, as well as proportions which indicate emotional relationships, are equally important if they serve the needs of our children. Neither is objectively better or worse, since both serve the child in his quest for freedom of expression.

Needless to say, most children fall between the two reactions with just a preference toward the one or the other.

MY CHILD WANTS TO EXPRESS "DISTANCE" AND "DEPTH"

If your child develops the desire to express distance and depth, he most probably is not the child who becomes emotionally involved in his art expression. Instead he is the type who uses his eyes for observation and likes to depict environment rather than experiences which involve the self. To develop a greater sensitivity for the characteristics

54a My child wants to express distance and depth. (See page 158) Courtesy Public Schools, Pittsburgh, Pa.

54b My child draws landscapes only. (See page 158) Courtesy Public Schools, Long Beach, Calif.

which create the feelings for depth and distance is the most that parents can contribute toward helping their children to master their desire. This should be done at any situation which lends itself to it. "Johnny, what makes the airplane appear so small way up in the air? . . . Yes, it's the distance. What would happen if it flew nearer and nearer toward you? It would appear to grow larger and larger. Is this the only change you would recognize? . . . You're right. When it was far away, you couldn't see any details, and it was all the same color. When it comes closer, you see more details, and can differentiate different colors." Next time, when you go out on a hike, you can do the same with a mountain, or a house in a landscape. In this way, you gradually make him conscious of the changing quality of distant objects in regard to size, details, and color. Next time when he paints and complains that his painting does not show enough distance, you can refer to his actual experiences. "Look at your painting, Johnny. Do you think your house in the foreground as compared to the house in the background is as different as we have seen it on our last hike? Let's find out! Is it different in size, different in the kind of details, and different in color? How about the road which leads to it? Has it the same width in the foreground of your painting as it has in the background? Can you see more details in the foreground? Is the color more differentiated?" The more sensitive your child grows toward these differences in appearance, the more easily will he master them (Figs. 54a and 54b).

Children are often so impressed by the first discovery of their ability to master distance and depth in their pictures that it takes away all other considerations for their painting. Only gradually may they recapture mood and atmosphere. Since this is an essential part of any identification with their own pictures, we must be careful that they do not lose their feeling for individual interpretations. Questions such as: "Johnny, was this a sunny day? Was it hot? Did you feel happy? Was it depressing? Was it misty? Was it clear?" would remind him of *his* relationship to his environment.

It cannot be emphasized enough that the best motivation for art activities takes place whenever there is occasion during every-day living. It consists mainly of making the child more sensitive toward his environment. This is the task of parents, and it cannot be replaced in school or elsewhere. The teacher cannot make the child sensitive during an art lesson if parents do not do their part at home! The teacher can only support the parent and can give the "technical help" in bringing out *what is in the child*. If the child has not grown up in a sensitive environment, then there is very little which can be brought out.

MY CHILD IS ONLY INTERESTED IN "EXPRESSION"

As has been said before, there are children who carry a world of their own with them. Environment has significance only if it is meaningful to them. Distance has no meaning in their pictures. On the contrary, for Mary the remoteness of a wish may make it more intense and more important, and therefore in her painting it may appear large. Mary is more interested in people, their expressions and her relationship to them. Whenever she paints something, it expresses a definite emotional feeling. Often it is not readily recognizable, but for her it is important. Nothing appears "real"; she does not care for "good proportions" nor for pleasing colors. However, she concentrates intensely on her paintings, and is apparently very absorbed in them (Fig. 55).

Since her emotional experiences are the driving components in her creative work, Mary needs your support and motivation in her subjective relationships to her environment. The most important contribution to her art will be your continuous interest in making her relationships more sensitive. "Mary, did you notice the people living in these shacks? How would you feel if you had to live in them? Did you see the old woman sitting on the doorstep? Do you think she was tired? What does her life consist of? When you were tired yesterday, where did you feel it most? Look at the people; they are having a picnic. Isn't it wonderful how absorbed they are in eating?" Next time Mary paints a painting of herself being tired and she is not satisfied with the expression, you can remind her of the different ways that people can be tired. You can compare her feeling of her "heavy head," of her "tension in the forehead," with her painting. "Does your painting show the heavy feeling of your head? Does it show the tension of which you spoke?" Needless to say, subjective feelings are always more difficult to control and motivate than things which can be seen. The important factor, however, is that Mary feels as much encouraged in *her* type of expression as Johnny feels in his.

For you as a parent, it is most important to know that both types of expression are equally important if they serve the needs of your child. Never try to convert one child's expression to another. Remember that the world consists of individuals, and the more freely they can unfold their own potential abilities, the happier they will be and the more secure they will feel in their own abilities.

55 My child is interested only in expression, and frequently "distorts" what he draws or paints. (See page 159) Courtesy Public Schools, Long Beach, Calif.

MY CHILD FREQUENTLY DISTORTS WHAT HE DRAWS OR PAINTS

Distortions are a basic means of expression not only in child art but also in most of the expressive works of great art. This is not only true for the representation of the figure but also for the representation of space. We have seen that for the eye, distant objects appear smaller. In visual representations distant objects are drawn in diminished size. If your child were to draw a distant tree as large as a tree in the foreground, you would probably say it was distorted. It only appears distorted if we regard the visual experience as the basic experience. For many people, including perhaps your child, it is not. If, for instance, the touch experience is the basic experience, as it is for the blind, the distant tree would never appear smaller to the sense of touch. You may walk miles and miles, and the sizes of trees do not change to the sense of

56 "The View from My Window." My child feels like a spectator, always looking at things. (See page 163) Courtesy Chicago Public Schools.

57 "Self portrait." My child feels involved in what he paints. (See page 163)
Courtesy Public Schools, Grand Rapids, Mich.

touch. The visual experience of diminished sizes for distant objects is then completely wrong for the sense of touch. In fact, the diminished size of distant objects constitutes a complete distortion for the sense of touch.

Distortions are not only relative to our senses, they are also relative to our emotions. What to the eye seems large may be completely insignificant to our emotions, and vice versa. If an accident were to occur to one of your beloved friends or relatives, and if it were at the foot of a mountain or near a skyscraper, there would be no space for the mountain or the skyscraper in your mind. Both would be dwarfed by the deep experience of the accident. Yet to the eye the proportion between the skyscraper and the human being has not changed. To paint it "out of proportion" would be a distortion to the eye but in line with your emotions.

Thus we have seen that "distortions" may only look like distortions, but may actually be meaningful expressions to your child.

Before you criticize distortions, be sure that you are not imposing your own one-sided visual concept upon your child. You can easily find out whether your child is disturbed by his "distorted" forms or whether they serve his expression. If he does not follow visual characteristics, but emphasizes expression in his work, you can be sure that his distortions are as meaningful to him as "correct" proportions may be to you. If he does not feel like a spectator, *looking* at things, but *feels* involved in his experiences, what appears to you as distortion may be *the basic concept of his art* (compare Figs. 56 with 57).

MY CHILD PAINTS "ABSTRACT PAINTINGS,"

BUT I CAN'T SEE ANYTHING IN THEM

Don't worry, you don't have to see anything in them. "Abstract paintings" do not represent anything (Fig. 58). Like music, they may express something to which you react in your own way. If you listen to a piece of music and you don't happen to like it, that is no indication that the music necessarily is of poor quality. You may not be in the right mood or you may not be able to follow it, that is, identify yourself with the music. However, as soon as you can feel "something" in the music which comes close to your own past or present experiences,

58 My child paints what she calls "abstract." (See page 163)

the music will appeal to you. This may be through a meaningful rhythm, a melody which recalls some memories, or through a mood which may suddenly reveal itself. If you, however, are accustomed to listening to music, or have penetrated even more deeply into the nature of music, then you will know that tunes have their own lives, just as human beings do. They may be slow-moving and calm; they may be unpredictable and exciting; they may be joyous, or they may be sad. They may meet other tunes, and, like friends, be in harmony with them, or they may be fighting them in discords. They may lose themselves and may scarcely be recognizable when they appear again, or they may gloriously and triumphantly end in a "finale."

Colors and lines may have their own lives, too. A line may be calm, like the horizontal line in a peaceful evening landscape; a line may be unpredictable, and excitingly change its direction like a lightning flash in a thunderstorm; a line may go busily from one point to another, as though its aims were predetermined; a line may also go loafing around, as we do if we have nothing definite in mind. If one line meets another, it can be "angry" with it, or be so overpowering in its intensity that it scarcely leaves the previous line alive. Indeed, one can scarcely see it, so much has it been "intimidated." Two lines may also "walk together" in perfect harmony. Also, a color "may feel" fine or disgusted. When does red feel fine, bright, and glorious? When does it feel dull and disgusted? But red, just like you, can meet a friend. What color is a "friend" of red? Red can be in harmony with its friend or it can fight the friend. It can be triumphant and glorious, or can walk almost unrecognized in the "shadow" of other colors. Such can be the life of colors. They do not need to represent "something." Like music, *they may have their own lives.*

When your child paints an "abstract painting," he may have no such considerations in his mind. But unconsciously they are present. Your child may simply "dabble" with color. However, by experimenting with colors and by arranging them in certain blobs or patterns, he learns of their reactions, he finds new mixtures. Thus, he discovers their attributes and unconsciously identifies with them. Your child may not even follow a definite mood. However, through the distribution of colors and relationships which he creates on paper, he may not only end up with a very distinct expression, but he may also grow in his feeling for organization.

If your child paints what he calls "abstract paintings," and you can't see anything in them, don't worry; he will go out and discover the life of lines, shapes, and colors as a part of the creative and investigatory spirit which is so vital for his future life.

THE MEANING OF MODELING DURING THIS PERIOD

Modeling has a very distinct meaning during this period because it often helps the child who strives for "perfection" and who has lost confidence in his own abilities to regain his creativeness. The reason for it can be found in the fact that in modeling there is no change from the three-dimensional perception of depth and distance to the two-dimensional representation on the paper that there is in painting. Most of the disappointments during this period of development are created by the child's technical inability to express what he imagines. Part of this difficulty in painting is due to the transition from a three-dimensionally conceived environment into a two-dimensional expression on the paper. Such a change is not necessary in modeling. A three-dimensionally conceived object remains three-dimensional in its final representation in clay. Because of this, children who become more critical of their final products may more easily overcome this critical awareness in modeling. This directness of expressing experiences in clay can be further fostered by encouraging the child to model a motion step by step as it is actually experienced. For instance, the clay figure can go through the motion of sitting down. "Johnny, when you were tired, how did you sit?" Johnny could first model the standing figure and then, by going through the motions, gradually bring the figure to the desired position. This would not only produce a final product which he can appreciate, but would also promote a close relationship between his work and himself. Such a feeling of self-identification is most desirable because only through it can the child gain confidence in his expression. The more the desire to express his own experiences grows, the less will he be concerned with external perfection.

In modeling too, we shall see that there are children who are more concerned with expression and others who are more concerned with the appearance of their sculpture. The child who predominantly seeks to express his emotions and feelings in his sculpture most likely sacrifices the smoothness and "pleasing" surface treatment to the expressiveness of his work. His sculpture may be "ugly" to us. But it would be completely wrong to impose our aesthetic feelings upon him. This would not only be meaningless to him but would also inhibit his mode of expression. As we have said previously, it is the experience through which your child grows regardless of the appearance of the final product. However, there are also children who emphasize the surface treatment, the appearance of their final product. For them correct proportion and often realistic likeness become essential. He may find them more easily in his clay work than in his painting, especially if his confidence is somewhat shaken. In his modeling, the roundness of the sculpture is a part of the process. In painting, this three-dimensional quality must first be introduced. This makes it much more difficult for the child to concentrate on appearance, because so much more additional effort has to be spent merely in mastering the technical ability to produce depth in a painting.

From what has been said, it is evident that both types of expression are equally important if they serve the child's needs. Whether a child concentrates more on the expression of emotions and feelings or on the appearance of a sculpture, most important remains the fact that he grows through his experiences whenever they help in his individual expression (Figs. 59a and 59b).

59a My child likes to carve in plaster.

59b My child finds modeling easier than painting. (See page 166)

MY CHILD IS NOT INTERESTED IN ART

As your child grows, he becomes more critical toward his work. Often this critical awareness overpowers his desire to express himself creatively. This is especially true in children who move quickly from childhood into adolescence. If this change from one stage to another occurs in too short a time, the child cannot adjust to his critical awareness quickly enough, and becomes unsatisfied with his creative work. He considers everything as childish and "not good." If this occurs too often and nothing is done about it, he loses interest in art and stops his work altogether. He can't draw anything because through his sudden critical awareness he realizes the inefficiency of his childish approach. The expression in drawing may seem childish and often as ridiculous to him as childish games like hide-and-seek appear to his "mature" attitude.

The problem is how to make the change to maturity a gradual one. Parents can help very much in stimulating the child consciously to appreciate his own achievements. "Johnny, tell me, how did you get this stormy sky? What colors did you use?" Johnny may be completely unaware of his own achievements. However, by leading him to the discovery of his own achievements and by bringing them to his consciousness, we have helped him to move from a stage of accidental production to a stage of more conscious achievement. By becoming conscious of the colors he mixed into a stormy sky, Johnny will be able not only to repeat the performance but also to control it. "Mary, tell me, what did you do to make your house look that distant?" A discussion with Mary will soon reveal to her in detail what she actually did. It will bring to her consciousness that she has drawn the distant house relatively smaller than objects in the foreground. She may also discover that she painted the distant colors duller and less intensively than the colors which she used in the foreground. Such self-awareness raises the conscious level of her creative achievements and thus helps her to consciously master her technical skills. It is self-understood that such motivations of making the child more conscious of his own achievements must never occur during the creative process. There they would greatly interfere with the intuitive character of your child's art. This motivation must always occur after the child has finished his product.

The older the child grows, the more the parent can support only what the child actually should experience in school. The child's needs for a greater variety of techniques and skills can scarcely be satisfied at home. A child who is not interested in art shows that he has not had enough satisfying experiences in creative expression. Very often a good workshop for boys where they can engage in tinkering may do wonders during this period of development. The important meaning of techniques and skills for the development of your child will be discussed in the following chapter.

THE MEANING OF TECHNIQUES AND SKILLS FOR THE DEVELOPMENT OF MY CHILD

In order to prevent the child from being discouraged by his "childish" products, it is necessary that certain skills and techniques be introduced. They will enable the child to appreciate a product which he otherwise would have neglected or even ridiculed. In countless cases I have seen children appreciate linol cuts of designs which they never would have accepted in drawings or paintings. In linol cuts the design is cut with a cutting tool into linoleum, and from there printed on paper (Fig. 60b). The transition of a pencil drawing into a celluloid engraving sometimes does wonders. Technical skills become an essential part of creative expression at this period. The introduction of new art media becomes a vital stimulus at a time when the child needs the assurance that he can consciously master a problem which can stand his critical awareness. It is, however, most important for parents to know that *their* critical attitude toward their children's work only increases the child's lack of confidence. The child is still a child, and his desire for increased skill does not mean adult perfection. It is here that we usually make the greatest mistakes. Being "encouraged" by the child's changed attitude toward his final product and his greater demand for skills, we often forget to realize that the child is far from being an adult. Art expression on all levels is highly individual. Perfection means something entirely different for him; at this stage it is simply a realization of the significance of his final product. He has never before considered the outcome of his creative expression as important. He was always tied up with the process of doing things in the same way, just as he was also satisfied with playing for its own sake. Now he wants to achieve a final product

60a   There are many other media of art expression, such as constructions.   (See page 172)

60b   Linol cut or other printing processes give much satisfaction to the child. (See page 172)

60c Puppetry.

60d Scratchboard drawing, a simple technique where the child covers a smooth board with black ink and scratches out the drawing. Such technical procedures help the child in overcoming his critical awareness. (See page 172)

in much the same manner that he likes to have rules attached to his games. His interest has shifted from the process to the final outcome. That does not mean that the final outcome must be "perfect." On the contrary, the more you can encourage your child to remain experimental, that is, to try many different approaches, the more will he become flexible and creative. (Figs. 60a, b, c, d)

HOW DOES ADOLESCENCE AFFECT MY CHILD'S ART?

Adolescence can be characterized as the stage in human development which is between childhood and adulthood. It begins with characteristic changes of the functions of the sex organs both in boys and in girls. These changes are usually accompanied by a greater consciousness of the significance of the maturing body and mind. This greater awareness of the self places the individual in a different, more conscious and critical relationship to his environment; also, creative activity is greatly affected by these changes. Since creative activity is a part of the imaginative activity of the child in general, the imaginative activity of the child is also greatly affected by these changes. As has been pointed out previously, this difference in imaginative activity expresses itself best in the different ways in which children and adults play. Children play without awareness of their actions, using their imaginations to make up for what reality does not provide. The adolescent, too, has outgrown the stage in which he uses symbols (such as a block or a stick) to substitute for reality; however, his imagination is not yet as clearly defined as the imagination of the adult. In his games he refrains from using such oversimplified or abstract symbols. In life, however, he most often adheres to unreal, dramatized, romantic concepts. At a particular stage he wants to become a cowboy or a forest ranger, with no other desire but the one of following his romantic ideals. His preferences in literature and movies point in the same direction. This all gives ample evidence that the adolescent individual is by no means a realist who deals with facts and who lives in an objective world. On the contrary, the adolescent most often has a tendency to withdraw from reality and live in a world of his own.

In his art he is too "self-critical" to accept child standards. Yet we must not make the mistake of moving too far in the direction of professionalism. The drawing or painting of still-lifes such as "a bottle and a lantern," or any other variations still in common practice in schools, will definitely not help his desire for romance and adventure. During this period, most forming and important in human development, art can only be effective if it meets the needs of the growing adolescent. Above all, it must provide him with opportunities for expression of *his* ideas and emotions. The child must, without imposed perfection, be motivated and encouraged to *experiment* in materials and art media in his own striving for "adventures" and discoveries. Adolescents have a real need to express themselves, whether it is in art, music, writing, dramatics, or dancing.

However, if we neglect these specific needs of the adolescent and emphasize perfection at too early a stage, the child, unable to achieve his goal, and frustrated in his desire for experimentation, will cease his creative ambitions altogether. This is too often the effect of adolescence on art. It is of great importance that parents be aware of their mission in encouraging their adolescent children in their own form of expression by not emphasizing or imposing their own concepts of perfection. Only then shall we be able to keep art as an important vehicle of growth beyond the stage of childhood.

WHAT MATERIALS SHOULD MY CHILD HAVE?

As the child becomes more mature, his need for a greater variety and complexity of expression grows. This is especially true for this period of greater awareness in which skills and techniques become increasingly important. The child should therefore have a greater variety of materials at his disposal. Materials which promote the use of tools and the application of skills are often of great importance for the overcoming of inhibitions toward "childlike" results. Carving and cutting tools for linoleum or wood cuts are most desirable for this age. Even a kit for etching or engraving will be a welcome present. Water colors will still serve a good purpose. Oil paints, with their great flexibility and adaptability in their usage, are also an excellent medium. Since the child during this stage of development derives much satisfaction from a final product, art materials which easily produce effects, like oil paint, linol cuts, celluloid engravings, or etchings are very desirable. If your child wishes to make his own oil paints, he can take paint pigment in powder form and mix it with linseed oil to a paste-like consistency. If he puts his different colors in small preserve glasses and "seals" them with water, his paint will remain fresh underneath the water. A limited number of colors will encourage the child to mix his own hues and shades. It should, however, be kept in mind that at all times the use of materials and their selection remain extremely personal.

my child seems especially gifted to me

THROUGHOUT this book nothing has been said about special gifts or talents. We have talked only about children who are free, less free, or inhibited, and who show these personality characteristics in their creative work. It has also been demonstrated how creative work is influenced by growth, and conversely. This was done out of the deep conviction that creative expression is for *all* children and not for a selected group. While some children express themselves more easily than others, we shall only speak of "talent" or "special gift" if the creative product becomes a vital part of a conscious desire for creation. This usually occurs with the oncoming of adolescence. It is most often during this period that the child reveals his special feeling and ambitions for art.

If parents discover such drives in their children, it is important to pay *special* attention to them. Artistic talent is a rare gift with which not many individuals are blessed. To neglect it would not only mean unhappiness on the part of your child, but would be wrong on your part. One of the basic differences between man and animal is that men create and the animal does not. If this quality, in its highest form, that of artistic talent, remains unused or neglected, one of the greatest contributions of man to society remains unfostered or undeveloped. It is therefore one of our highest duties toward our children and toward society to contribute to the development of artistic ability by whatever means we can. So many of our children do not know what to choose for their vocational goals. Sincere interests are rare. The dilemma is great when children are often forced to make decisions with regard to their future profession too early in their lives. Any talent with which a child is endowed by nature should be a welcome guide to parents. But remember, skills and techniques are not enough for artistic expression! In fact, if you overemphasize the meaning of them, it may only be harmful to your child. I have seen many parents thinking of their children as little geniuses because they could draw perspective correctly, or a figure in "correct" proportions. Remember, too, that talent is not something which you or I determine. It must be in the child, and it is rarely difficult to detect it. It is a drive which takes possession of the child, and you can see whether your child merely uses his skills or is really absorbed in his work. If your child not only loves art but also spends much of his free time in creating in art media, it is important that you support his drive. Whether he will use it for his own sake or for future vocational aims should not enter your thoughts at this time. Even if art remains only a lifelong companion to whom your child can turn whenever the need arises, you have given him an invaluable friend and have enriched his life in large measure. Above all, we never know how important this friend may become in times of storm and stress. But even at the present time, the utmost should be done to give your child the best opportunity to develop his talent.

The home can provide only a part of the necessary stimulation which a gifted child needs. Your positive and encouraging attitude is the greatest help the child can get from you. If you in addition provide him with the necessary art materials, you have done the best you can do. Of course, it is necessary that you consult with your school authorities. The art teacher will always be glad to help you. If there are "art classes" in your town, or an art school, your child may want to participate in them. However, be careful not to overstimulate your child. His reactions are always the best guide to what you should do in the realm of art education. Creative activities can never be forced upon children; they must develop from their own desires for expression. Overstimulation, growing from the drive of eager parents to do the "best" for their children, has often killed the child's urge for artistic expression. A child who is really gifted does not need to be reminded to use his creative energies. He will do so because of his natural drive, and will be grateful for the support you give him.

how is my child's future
affected by his art?

PSYCHOLOGISTS agree that the most basic influences in our lives occur during early childhood. Not only is our personality formed during this important period, but also most of the trends for our further development. It is not an exaggeration to say that it is basically our childhood experiences which determine whether we live in fear, frustrated, shy, and inhibited, full of feelings of inferiority, or whether we live basically free, uninhibited, and well adjusted for the rest of our lives. It is self-evident that we are exposed to many external influences, to many happenings which occur in our lives and which we cannot influence. In most instances it is, however, our attitude toward these happenings, our ability to adjust to them, to accept them and "make the best of them," or to reject them and be frustrated, which determines our state of mind. The foundation for this attitude in most individuals is laid in early childhood. I have often heard people say: "What was good enough for my father is good enough for me. He never had any art training, and I haven't missed it." Such statements not only reject progress, but completely deny the fact that we are living in a world of confusion in which people cannot get along with one another. It further denies the fact that a shockingly large number of our population suffers at one time or another from acute mental illness. The staggering number of nervous breakdowns, and of people with adjustment difficulties, is ample evidence for the need for every possible means which we can muster to provide our children with the best opportunities for developing a healthy personality. That art has a fundamental influence on the child's personality growth, and therefore also on his future, is a fact which has been determined beyond any doubt. Not only does it influence the child's ability for emotional adjustment, it also provides him with avenues to make his life richer and more beautiful. His sensitivity toward perceptual experiences, such as observing, hearing, touching, as well as his discovery of what is beautiful, will greatly contribute to his life. Above all, in every phase of his life he will either use his inventive, creative approach, or he will depend on imitating given patterns. We should not forget that what makes a physician, an engineer, a physicist, a businessman, an architect, or a carpenter successful is his inventive power, a power that makes him look at his profession as a never ending source for new discoveries and changes. Whatever profession your child chooses, he will need the creative attitude which he has achieved through his art. Any worker, whether he uses his mind or his manual skills, or both, is lost if he merely depends on blind obedience in the imitation of a given pattern. We must never forget that much of our happiness depends on our ability to use and take advantage of the many opportunities which this life offers.

As a citizen your child must not fail to realize that one of the very basic essentials in a democratic society is to live at peace with his neighbors, to regard them as individuals, each in his own right, and to cooperate with them. All these attributes are not only stressed in art but are an essential part of it. As your child engages in creative activities and develops his own freedom and initiative, he is brought up in the spirit of recognizing and appreciating individual differences. As he expresses himself independently as an individual, he also realizes that the same right belongs to others. As he concentrates on the subject matter which he expresses, he identifies himself with the things he creates. Thus he develops the feeling for others which is so essential in the world today. In group work, inspired by his creative urge, he engages in cooperation and learns to get along with others. Above all, as he creates, he continuously confronts himself with his own experiences and thus relieves himself of tensions and emotional stress, so important for his future well-being. However, art not only serves as an emotional outlet but as a continuous source of enjoyment in which the child organizes his thoughts and feelings in creative media. It is this ability to organize which changes chaos into order and meaninglessness into meaningfulness.

VOCATIONAL POSSIBILITIES

Up to this point, art has been discussed only in its general implications for the growth of our children. In what follows, a brief account will be given to those who are interested in pursuing art as their future vocation. No attempt will be made to give a thorough discussion of the vocational possibilities in art. This is intended much more as a guide for parents in helping their children to clarify their thinking when they arrive at the period in which they have to make decisions with regard to their special preparation for their future vocation.

We shall discuss the main prerequisites which are necessary for five major vocational possibilities connected with art. They are: (1) free-lance art; (2) art teaching; (3) any form of commercial or applied art; (4) art history and curating of art museums; (5) art therapy.

The Free-Lance Artist

A free-lance artist is an artist who creates on his own without being regularly employed. The usual preparation is done either in art schools or in fine-arts departments in colleges.

It is indeed very unfortunate that so very few artists in the United States can earn a living through their art products. This should, however, by no means be the determining factor for parents in helping their children in making their decisions. The determining factor must always remain the child's own drive and talent. Parents who are sensitive toward their children can "feel" whether the drive of their children is a genuine and persistent one. There is no reason whatsoever to encourage a child to become an artist if the child does not have a very strong desire for it. Remember, to be an artist is not an easy or romantic profession. It implies great sacrifices. Before you encourage your child to take up an artistic career, your child must above all be creative; he must have talent, skill, and perseverance. None of these attributes can be absent. However, if it is necessary to dispense with one, it is that which commonly is considered the most important—skill. Skill, if it is not present at the beginning, develops with the urge for expression, if this urge is present. In fact, it often proves to be of great benefit if skill has to be "conquered." It would not be difficult at all to show quite a number of examples in which too much skill stood in the way of the development of a sincere art expression. I have seen many children who, because of their highly developed skills, did not arrive at the depth and sincerity which is essential to a work of art. It often happens that skill develops rapidly and "outdoes" the other qualities. Yet, most commonly, skill is regarded as the most important factor for an artist.

To become an artist is one of the decisions for which the child does not need any external motivation. The child, and the child only, must be the decisive factor. The sensitive parent, however, can be of great help to him in his decision. He will best of all know how much and how deeply the child is involved in his art expression. He knows how much time the child is spending in art activities, and develops a good feeling for the importance which art has for his child. Never force the child into any artistic occupation because the child appears to you to be "talented." To be a free-lance artist is more than a mere profession. If your child does not feel the urgent drive to become one, there is no need for encouragement. On the other hand, if your child is convinced of his mission as an artist, he will need your support. It is one of your highest moral obligations not to counteract your child's drive because of material or other considerations, but to help your child to place his artistic power at the disposal of man.

The Art Teacher

The prerequisites necessary for a good art teacher are greatly misunderstood. The common notion that an art teacher must be an artist is just as wrong as the notion that one who cannot be an artist can still become an art teacher. To be a teacher means to be sympathetic and understanding to human problems. It should be frankly stated that one who cannot succeed as an artist should try another job rather than go into art teaching if he does not have a special desire to become a teacher. A frustrated artist most likely will not be inspiring to children. The best art teacher would be an artist who at the same time has a deep understanding of human problems and a great desire to help children and youth in their growth and development. The usual preparation for art teaching is done in departments of education or art education in colleges and art schools.

Depending on the level of teaching, the emphasis is on different factors. Teaching art to children involves more of the knowledge and psychological understanding of the needs of children than ability in skills and techniques. The teaching of art on the higher levels of learning presumes more specialized qualities on the part of the teacher.

There is scarcely a more rewarding job than that of helping young people to grow and to develop their creative potentialities. If your child thinks of becoming an art teacher because he is interested in children, their development, and their creative expression, by all means encourage him in his desire. He should know that art in the elementary classroom is used as an important means for the total development of the child. This book, I hope, has given you some indication and evidence of it. If your child, therefore, chooses to become an art teacher in public schools, he must first of all have a sincere interest in children, and secondly in creative processes.

If your child is more interested in older children, that is, in children on the high-school level, his preparation must be still more concerned with a more general and broad background in the arts, and the effect of these arts on the individual, than with specialized art skills and techniques. While he does not need to have special artistic skill, it will be essential for him to create in different art media, for only through his own experiences will he be able to gain insight into the nature of creating in different art media. However, it is by no means essential that your child acquire these skills in high school. Even if he has no visible talent but has a strong desire to help children develop through art you should encourage him in his desire to become an art teacher. He will acquire the essential skills during his college preparation.

Only when your child has special artistic abilities and in addition likes young people should he be encouraged to teach art in fine-arts departments or art schools.

There is a very great need for good art teachers, especially in elementary and high schools. According to latest reports, there are more open positions by far than there are available art teachers. The situation is growing worse with the increasing number of elementary-school children. This, however, should by no means be the determining factor in the selection of your child's future profession. His sincere interest in young people and in art must remain your main guide in helping him to choose his profession.

The Commercial Artist

The possibilities of applied or commercial art are almost unlimited in a time which depends so much on industrial design and advertisement. Television too has brought new opportunities into this fascinating field. Competition, however, is very great. If your child wants to become a commercial artist, he must have special abilities. I have seen many young people choose this profession because they have "some" talent, but it would not be enough to pursue a "fine arts" career. There is actually no need of making a distinction between the two. The commercial artist needs as much creative ability and skill as any other kind of artist. There are special art schools, and a few college art departments, which prepare for commercial art.

As has been said before, commercial art touches almost every part of our lives. Beginning with our homes, where countless applications of applied art can be encountered, from the design of kitchen utensils, such as refrigerators, gas stoves and silverware, to the interior design of furniture, fashion, and textiles, to the designs of cars and other forms of industrial applications, there is an almost inexhaustible field of activity for the commercial artist. If we add the vast field of advertising, including window display, lettering, poster art, typography, illustration, and cartooning, and the many areas which relate to the theater and movie production, such as stage design, scenery painting, and costume design, there is scarcely anything left which remains untouched by commercial art or industrial design.

In commercial art more than in any other area of artistic careers, skill and inventiveness is important. If your child is clumsy, he probably will not be able to withstand the enormous competition, unless he is extremely inventive. Since the commercial artist, especially the industrial designer, has to know the properties of a large number of materials, your child should show investigative interest in materials if he wants to make this his life profession. Parents, more than anyone else, will know whether their children have this investigative spirit in taking things apart and fixing or even inventing gadgets. But don't be too critical and don't expect perfection from your child. If your child is inclined to experiment and invent, and in addition shows interest in his field, he will develop the necessary perfection of his skills during his training in schools.

The whole field of crafts also belongs to the applied arts. Pottery has become of increasing interest during the last few years. Hand-made jewelry has again attracted much attention. Yet it should be kept in mind that it still remains a difficult task to succeed as a potter or jewelry designer even with much inventive power and skill.

No attempt to go into a more detailed discussion is made because it is assumed that parents will want to inform themselves more fully than is possible here if their children wish to choose a particular field of interest as their own career.

Art History and Curating Art Museums

The role which art museums are playing in community life is an ever increasing one. In many communities the art museum has become the center of cultural activities. It is not only the place where works of art are displayed for the benefit of the public, but it has also become the center for many other activities. It is by no means unusual for community concerts to be held in museums, and it has almost become an American custom to hold children's art classes in museums. Thus, the importance of museums has far outgrown the mere exhibition hall of historical art collections. It has become a living monument in American culture.

If your child is interested in art, its meaning and sources, he may want to work in a museum. If he also possesses, in addition to his inquisitiveness about art objects, the ability to organize and administrate, he might enjoy work in a museum. The preparation for museum jobs as well as for becoming art historians is usually done in fine-arts departments in colleges. Some universities offer special courses for museum work. It is needless to say that the number of jobs in museums is greatly limited by the relatively small number of museums.

Art Therapy

The use of art as therapy is a very recent application of art. As this book has shown you, art has a very definite relationship to the personality of its creator. These influences of art on the individual have therapeutic implications. One which can most easily be understood is the use of art as an emotional outlet. Just as you feel better if you talk over your problems instead of keeping them to yourself, the individual feels better if he can get rid of his tensions through art. In order to understand and interpret the phases of a therapeutic process, one has to study the psychological and therapeutic implication of the arts. There are special schools of occupational therapy which include art therapy.

If your child becomes interested in the psychological implications of art, in learning how to help people overcome their emotional difficulties, he may want to inform himself about the nature of this vocation. The main prerequisite is a profound interest in human problems. His own skill is of secondary importance. Although such skill is desirable, if for no other purpose than that of a better understanding in using art media, it is not essential except in the use of crafts in occupational therapy. Obviously, in order to apply weaving to therapeutic purposes, one has to know the skills related to it. Just as in any other occupation which deals with human beings, in addition to an interest in human problems, much patience and perseverance are necessary. I have seen many therapists fail only because they did not have enough patience with their clients. Changes often occur very gradually, almost unrecognizably for the untrained person. Sometimes no visible changes can be seen for a long time. Great perseverance and patience are essential qualities for an effective therapist. If your child does not have these qualities, he may not only be unhappy in this profession, but may be harmful to others.

A brief account has been given of the main vocations related to art. This has been done for the purpose of indicating to parents the opportunities for those who would like to choose art as a career. No attempt has been made to go into the details of any of the previously mentioned occupations, for to do so would not have been desirable within the framework of this book.

ART AS A HOBBY

The amateur artist, painter, potter, jewelry maker, craftsman, are all part of our contemporary art movement. The idea that anyone can create is one of the distinct contributions of our time. After all, one of the most important differences between man and animal is that man creates and the animal does not. To leave this great endowment unused would not only mean wasting a distinct attribute, but missing much of life's enjoyment.

The reader will have noticed that every effort has been made to save the child's creative abilities, and with them his flexibility, beyond adolescence. This was done not only with the hope that he might continue to be creative in life situations but also that he might use art as a form of active expression. Whether you start a pottery shop in your basement or whether you begin to express yourself in painting does not matter. What is of great importance is that you are actively engaged in creating something. Actually, the most important things are that you *start* and that you overcome the conventional idea that you have to know how to do things. Throw your "right's" and "wrong's" aside and start as sincerely as you can. After a short time of dabbling with oil paint or chalks, you will find it so exciting that you will get more and more involved in it. Most important, however, is that whatever you do should be *yours*! It is this genuine relationship to your own work that makes it meaningful to you. Do not accept methods which prescribe to you, step by step, what you have to do. Such methods are as remote from art as slavery is from freedom. They will not satisfy you because you will not find yourself in them. Whatever you do, even if it appears to you primitive in the beginning, it must be a part of yourself. Remember, the greatness of art as a hobby lies in its never ending possibilities for experimentation. It is this attribute of constantly approaching new situations with the desire to solve them which makes art so exciting. Don't use the standards of others. Don't look to see how others have made what you intend to make. Don't compare your work with theirs. The standards of others are always detrimental to your own expression. Accept yourself as you are, and grow and improve on the basis of your *own* experience. Don't be impatient and don't push yourself. Don't imitate merely for imitation's sake. We are all influenced by what we see, and especially by what appeals to us. Such influences become a part of us, whether we want them to or not. However, purposely to imitate not only means giving up one's own personality; it also means denying oneself the privilege of creating as an individual.

Never say it is too late for you. In countless cases I have had the great privilege of seeing individuals of *all* ages turn to art and grow with it as one of the greatest companions in life.

It makes no difference what you start with. It may be that you start with "doodling" in colors and lines and suddenly discover exciting mixtures and color relationships. You may end with something that you can't even describe; it may be a dance of colors, or the whirling foliage on a stormy day. Or you may want to begin with something you have once seen, or felt.

The greatest value of art as a hobby is in your total absorption in it. Art is not satisfied with any part of yourself. It needs you as a whole. It is this attribute of art which pulls you out of your daily routine. It prevents you from getting tense and falling into a rut. Above all, it shows new avenues for experience which, once you have started to try them, open up new vistas through the never ending possibilities of new and exciting experiments. Last but not least it may be one of the best ways of learning to appreciate what creative activity may mean to your child.